INNOCENCE OF A CHILD

INNOCENCE OF A CHILD

by

DE'RON SMITH

Publishing Co.: D-Inspirational Publishing, Cincinnati, Ohio

ISBN: 978-0-6152668-6-2

Designed by Vince Pannullo
Book edited by Cindy Gallagher

Printed in the United States of America by
One Communications US. LLC 800-621-2556 NYC

To contact our office regarding bulk orders, to schedule speaking events, or to assist in any intervention, please e-mail us at **info@dinspirationalpublishing.org**, visit our website at **www.idreamacademy.org**, or call us at **(513) 407-8984**.

CONTENTS

IN LOVING MEMORY

To my beloved Dad, Willie P. ("Rusty") Smith, Jr. who in the end was able to see my transition from boyhood to manhood. God's hands were on you until the end. You modeled manliness, and provided a true concept of determination, courage, and honor. You gave God your best and served as a diligent soldier completing your divine assignment. Your spirit will continue to live on through me, the rest of your family, as well as many others. Although this book can in no way measure up to the heavenly crown you now wear, I trust this will serve as a small token of my gratitude, appreciation, and love. You will be forever missed.

April 29, 1938 – December 18, 2007

Barbara ("Tootsie") King, Lisa R., Jessie Smith,
Mr. and Mrs. James Cardwell, John Dixon, and
Mr. Norman Brown

DEDICATIONS

I thank the Lord Jesus Christ for providing the strength I needed to write this book. Every opposition imaginable came against me; nevertheless "I can do all things through Christ who strengthens me!"

To my beloved mother, Elder Doris E. Smith, for all of the tears you've cried and the many, many miles you traveled to visit me. Your labor was not in vain; I love you so much!

To you, Dad, I am so proud of you; today you are evidence that change can take place! The things you contribute to this family are immeasurable; keep up the good work!

To all of my sisters and brothers, each of you played a very significant part in my success, especially you, Gwen (a.k.a. Gail), you amazed me. You were the last person I thought would stand by my side for seven long years. You never missed a beat!

To everyone who labored by my side while I went through different mood swings from frustration (smile). But true … thank you.

To my beloved son, Jibri, you've never ceased to make me proud! You are my heart, son, and I do all of this life turnaround for you!

Special Dedications

TO the entire Walker/Cardwell family, you have never said a negative word against me, thank you. Especially you Danelle, you really are sweet and a good mother. God will bless you with your heart's desire. Keep the faith!

To the Brown family, thank you!

To Gregory (a.k.a. Geggy), after all these years, we are still tight!

To everyone doing time in prisons all across our country, you can be somebody ... if you want to be! Don't let society dictate who you are. God can turn *all* of your negative experiences into something good! Be persistent in change, courageous in battle, and wise in your pursuit! You too can walk in victory!

I would like to extend an extra special thanks to Robert Bradley, Donna Favors-Davis, Valerie Weisner, and Professor Jeff Hillard.

PREFACE

LIFE is full of ups and downs, good decisions and bad decisions, growth, and death. Through it all, there is generally a desire to help others avoid some of the same mistakes that we have made, but the ability and/or the opportunity to help others sometimes gets hampered.

The Bible describes the conversation when God told Moses to be His spokesman. Moses countered by saying that He [God] should find someone else. Moses didn't see himself as a good speaker, but Moses had something to say. He had unique knowledge; he had unique experiences; he had a unique voice. Every man has a voice, and for a man to speak his true voice takes courage. For some, that voice may come across as well learned or unlearned. But the spirit of a person's heart transcends the conventions of particular styles of speech and literary commonalities. In my book, *Innocence of a Child*, I have put aside fear and have spoken from my heart as I tell my experiences ranging from innocence lost to innocence regained to innocence shared. Life moves in stages; what doesn't grow, doesn't have life. The growth of my voice is felt in these pages.

This is not a stuffy, literary piece of nonfiction, nor is it a haphazard compilation of thoughts brought together for the sake of producing a book. As you read *Innocence of a Child*, you will see that my particular style of writing is created to let you understand me and my thinking process through my language. I purposefully took certain license with grammar and spelling so that you can enter into my world.

Come with me; enter my world and my life as I take you on a trip through the *Innocence of a Child*.

THE MOLDING PROCESS

"… Suffer the little children to come unto me, and forbid them not — For of such is the kingdom of God…"

—Mark 10:14

THE laughter turned into fear as our day ended from playing outside. Fear from knowing that the very moment my tiny hand turned the doorknob to enter the home, my world would change. As soon as I stepped across the threshold, it would be like entering the *Twilight Zone*, and the security the outdoors offered would disappear, leaving no one to protect me from the misery inside.

The outdoors was my sanctuary—a big world filled with space, allowing me to release a scream if I wanted to with nothing said about it—*my* world! A place where there were no restrictions, where I could let my innocence have rule. But the inside wasn't so. The restrictions began as soon as I entered. "No eating in the living-room; No lying on the couch, sit on it! You want to lay on something, that's what your bed is for…" my dad authoritatively spoke in his deep, southern voice.

I was born December 24, 1967, the seventh child. That made four girls and three boys at the time, that is, until Mom and Dad decided to bring one more child into the equation—Sharon, another girl, just what I needed!

Growing up as kids, I'm sure we've all had someone with whom we would team up, sort of a Lone Ranger and Tonto, so to speak. Well, my Tonto's name was Gregory, but since that word was a bit difficult for me to pronounce, I nicknamed him Geggy. He was a tall, thin kid, eight months older than I, and me: short in stature with pointed ears and a fiery temper some referred to as "troll-like"—we were inseparable.

It was unknown to any of our parents the mischievous activities we engaged in. Although at the end of our day, when the parents had given the loud yell for us to come inside, our worlds would dramatically change. I wanted desperately to go with him, and often wished that his mom and dad could rescue me and take me as their own.

I can't say for certain what went on within the confines of his home, but in mine, Mom and Dad were drinking, partying, and fighting, and so were the kids. Madness was everywhere, fatherly advice absent, and a hug or a kiss was unthinkable. However, there was one area well demonstrated and esteemed to be very important in order for a person to pass from boyhood to manhood, or from girlhood to womanhood, and that key ingredient was **Party!**

I guess it was by fate that my placement in the line-up just happened to fall in the number seven slot; seven being God's perfect number, Mom would later come to say. Sharon and I were fortunate to have come through the birth canal during later times in life: times when Mom and Dad were *almost* at the end of their escapades of wild partying and physically abusing each other. But for a seven- or eight-year-old boy trapped in the middle of a war, almost seemed like an eternity.

Sharon never had the opportunity to fully understand the wild house-party flings and midnight fights that followed, but I wouldn't be so lucky. In the few years that I did manage to catch sight of their obtrusive living, their fighting, constant arguing, and flat-out evil temperament—possibly from hangovers—it was more than enough to deposit into the life of a child a bad attitude—and a bad attitude I did have.

It was inside the classroom where I best acted out my frustration, hitting other kids and disrespecting the teachers, even to the extent that I received a suspension until my parents came to conference—I was only in the first grade.

Yet, there was no act of frustration projected in any direction more than it was towards Sharon—I punished her. It was only necessary for me to inject upon someone the manner of treatment I received, mainly from Gail and Little Man. It wasn't that I lived to punish her, just that I didn't know any other way to express my anger; abuse was all I knew. When you were angry, striking your target was your release valve. Sure, I felt bad afterwards, but for the moment hitting her served its purpose.

It was stated that the unacceptable conduct stemmed from my home environment. Dad was a weekend drinker, although he didn't hesitate to make up for each weekday missed. Mom, who went along with the flow of things in hopes to keep peace, surrendered to the upcoming weekends due to encountering an exhaustive work week.

Make no mistake about it, I enjoyed watching the older folks dance and stumble from place to place, although my favorite pastime was going from person to person soliciting money. I learned from my older brothers and sisters that those caught up in the moment of partying became extremely generous after a few drinks of hard liquor and the music soothed them. Unfortunately, the party ended, and the happy expressions on both their faces gave way to the midnight madness that always followed and the painstaking fears I passionately dreaded.

Once again, violence filled the empty atmosphere, dismissing the happy moments as if they never even took place. What to expect had become repetitious. Screams would last throughut the night. Moreover, if luck wasn't on our side, the morning too would receive all of what was unable to be resolved the night before.

The pillow offered no help in blocking the shouts that penetrated my ears. Saddened by the sounds of frightening screams from Mom's voice, and the fact of my inability to help her, I tucked my head beneath the covers as if they were to carry me into another realm. Underneath, I could hear the pounding of my accelerated heartbeat, while scenes of envisioning to one day kill the man who was inflicting such abuse upon my mother made the night appear to have no end.

I couldn't hold back the tears that pressed their way across my face. I tossed and turned, swearing in harmony with my emotions never to become like the monster in the other room. I imagined how

I would be different with my wife and kids, especially my son—if I were to ever have one.

I prayed the new day would hurry, hoping it could bring with it a fragrance of calm to eliminate the memories of the night I just endured. At times, the new day did bring about an atmosphere of peace, partially projecting as if the events of yesterday were just an illusion. However, as much as I hoped for things to be completely pleasant, the wrath of Dad's everyday nature was still a factor. His callousness and overly authoritative attitude was injected upon everyone in the household and continued to produce an atmosphere of discomfort through exclaiming in his usual voice words of profanity and threats to anyone he believed unwilling to adhere unto his rules—no matter how absurd they were. It was his house, and not a day passed by where he failed to remind everyone of the fact—including Mom.

Entertaining the intoxicated crowd weekend after weekend was beginning to affect both of them. But before it could come to a complete end, I had to feed my curiosity of knowing what exactly it was that made everyone at the party feel so good. At age seven, I received instructions from my older brothers and sisters never to drink any dark liquor. I didn't understand why, and being such a young age, never thought to ask; therefore, I set search for anything with a light color to it and no cigarettes or whatever else possibly lying at the base of the glass.

It was the beginning! The beginning of encountering an entity that conquering would not come by easy victory. The beginning of paths created in my life in which, given another chance, I would not have taken. The beginning of losing *self*— that I may find *life*.

Two years later and the desire to host the festive events finally ceased. Dad was tired of the after-party trips to the precinct and Mom was tired of having her head bashed in by an overly intoxicated, weekend rebel. Whatever the reasons for the discontinuation, this gave us great relief in knowing there wasn't going to be an overcrowded and smoked-filled house upon the weekend to come. Another joy received was from knowing that possibly they weren't going to be fist fighting or throwing weapons thirty minutes afterward.

My father was a strong advocate for hard work, and anyone who did not work was viewed as a definite loser in his book, whereby Will, a.k.a. Little Man, ranked as chief example. I wanted to believe it was the alcohol transforming Dad into the beast my eyes beheld; however, the fact was, there wasn't a drop of alcohol in the house anymore. True, things had simmered down a bit, but the road that led to a happy home seemed light-years away. It was the verbal tormenting of each other. Daily something or another brought forth an argument, but the number-one reason was from the abuse he inflicted upon Little Man.

Mom cringed at the treatment he offered the children and was adamantly opposed to his choice of punishing tool—a long brown or black extension cord that was sure to leave memory marks. She hated that with a passion and often placed herself in the middle of every situation giving the appearance of inappropriateness. She hated all the more the fact that Little Man served as his own personal beating stick. Dad's response to everything was, "If you don't like it, you can get the hell out of my house;" his southern accent placing emphasis on the word *my*. My eldest two sisters, Cheryle, a.k.a. Bootsie, the eldest, and Debbie, the next eldest, who carried a wonderful quiet spirit, gladly gave him his wish.

A Change Must Come

MOM was determined to press toward change, and a change she was "going to receive, even if it killed her," she said. It was obvious the aftermath of what conspired between my parents in the former years still lingered in their souls. Each appeared to be somewhat reluctant to release the memories of hurt, pain, and abuse one infringed upon the other. The damages were done already. I suppose the impartations passed on to my brothers and sisters from witnessing so much of what Sharon and I were fortunate to have shared very little had rendered too implacable to mend. We strongly believed that this was the manner in which a person was expected to go through life; this was my reality.

No one received the proper nourishment one expects to receive from their parents, making it difficult to make appropriate decisions. Individuals lacking such essentials are most certain to intrude upon rough ground later down the road.

The answers to their problems lay at church, they believed. Attending on Sunday mornings, they were set with determination to embrace a new way of life; however, their Sundays weren't complete unless they dragged with them the three youngest of eight: Little Man, Sharon, and me.

This involvement in church was a good thing. It allowed for once in my life thus far to observe them doing something other than fight and party. I liked what I saw.

The transformation came much easier for Mom, it appeared. Not that she was ever mean or abusive towards any of us, but her way of doing things was different (hard to explain). I didn't know anything about Christianity, nor the rules of thumb listed in the Holy Bible. Yet there was one thing I was sure of: you weren't supposed to be evil—*mean,* if I would say. I was taught in Bible study class that Jesus was a loving God, one who cares and would not let any harm come to us.

On the contrary, it wasn't that simple for dear ole Dad. Whatever he possessed inside was unwilling to release him without a serious fight. He was just mean for no apparent reason it seemed, and I feared him immensely. Despite the fact that his attendance at church was something he honored and viewed as a step in the right direction, his conversion was unnoticeable. I asked Mom why he displayed so much anger towards us. Her reply was, "He doesn't know any better." I couldn't comprehend that logic, and for a child nine years of age that answer was far from acceptable.

Everyone managed to receive his or her own specialized share of Dad's wrath, whether it came by way of verbal (or in Little Man's case, physical) abuse. Nevertheless, not one person was excluded. I was heartbroken watching Dad torture my brother the way he had, simply being, Mom quotes, "his spittin' image."

We were lying comfortably on the living-room floor watching television one evening when out of nowhere Dad entered. For whatever reason—as if one was needed—he put his foot on my brother's neck. I heard a gasp squeeze its way from my brother's mouth. He was choking, I imagined. The curse of abuse had made its way into another generation whether knowingly or unknowingly.

I had thought the absence of alcohol would eliminate the problems plaguing my family but I could not have been more off base. The alcohol was only an escape from everything deposited inside of them, possibly from their childhoods. Neither of them ever discussed their upbringings.

Things could have been much worse, I suppose. But in my mind, I had received from the God of whom Mom spoke with such profound emotions the worst anyone could ever receive. I wasn't convinced anymore that there was a God who cared, watched over people, or loved them the way Mom said He does and would never allow harm to come upon those in His care. In addition to the incredulous thinking already induced, I wondered how someone so loving could sit by and watch while my mother had received so much abuse from my father in years past. If there was a God, I wondered, where was He in my life?

She tried insistently after her Sunday debut with the Lord to insert some spiritual guidance, expounding on the importance of prayer and trusting in God. "Trust?" I said, to myself: "I believe more in Santa Claus; at least the toys at Christmastime provide me with some type of truth. If this is God's way of protecting us, I'd rather protect myself."

It was difficult to trust when all I looked upon at such a young age was fighting, beatings of other members in my family, swearing of words I couldn't pronounce if I wanted to, neglect, and lack of intimacy. How was I ever supposed to believe that this God of hers had the power to change someone's life when from my observation on television kids all around the world and in my own downtown city streets were homeless, dying of hunger, and lying on concrete slabs? Not to mention, as soon as the church doors closed and we returned to our home, out of sight from the preacher and the other fake churchgoers, who also put up a front in hopes to appear holier than they actually were, all hell would break loose.

Moreover, I thought, what about Dad? I sincerely believed he was as mean now as in the days when the drinking and partying took place. And repeatedly I asked myself, where was the God that would stop him from beating Little Man senseless with an extension cord to the point he was apt to commit suicide, or from throwing everyone out of the house at the age of eighteen despite the fact they had never received parental guidance pertaining to the responsibilities of an adult? I wanted to know.

These questions barricaded me. What I saw far outweighed everything that was said. True, the house was no longer filled with obnoxious people looking to engage in a weekend thrill, nor was there any midnight bloodshed anymore; nevertheless, the screaming and constant arguing was just as bad, giving the home environment a display of little change—if any at all.

No one went through a weaning process. Instead, you and your belongings met the pavement once you reached the magic age. All of his six feet, two-inch frame spoke in his southern accented baritone voice that famous saying, "When you tuhn eighteen you gettin' the hell outta heah," never knowing the impact of his words nor the fear he was inducing inside of me. How could I live as a child, I thought, when I was being rushed into becoming a man?

It's Tougher Than I Thought

THE two distinctive attitudes still managed to collide more often than not. Dad, holding to his tenacious belief of "my way or the highway" attitude while Mom, doing her best to live the life of a devout Christian, began chastising him by way of biblical doctrine which made him even angrier, it appeared. Mom stated in fury how hard it was to live biblically steadfast in the word of God with so much opposition. "A change must come!" she exclaimed.

The fight for a peaceful home wouldn't come easily, she well knew. Nevertheless, she was determined to receive progress, if only a small piece. Her ambition to grow closer to the Lord took precedence over everything and everyone in her life, so much so that Bootsie, the eldest of eight, had to step in and take on the role of mom. She kept watch over us, since we were the youngest, providing me with the security I needed, security from being beat to death by my older brothers and sisters (mainly Gail, who hated me, and I hated her. We were like oil and water).

I received comfort from being held in Bootsie's arms as she rocked me to sleep after crying myself into a frenzy from wanting to go with Mom, knowing what was guaranteed to come my way once she was out of earshot. They wanted to distribute the beating they had been holding back for so long. They stated that I was a spoiled-rotten, whiny, little-bitty, pointed-ear brat. I didn't care what they thought about me and knew that as long as I was in the care of Bootsie, no one could do anything to me. If anyone laid a hand on me for whatever reason while she was gone, then everyone would pay.

She was indeed my guardian angel, ruthless, and they all knew it. Each one of my brothers and sisters possessed an evil streak in them. In fact, I truly believe, if confronted at the right time and right occasion, they would cause severe harm to someone (I guess it was only natural considering his or her habitat). Each of them displayed that side quite often, even my brother Tim, who is several years older than Little Man and third oldest of the eight.

As animals in the wild learn certain survival techniques to ensure their safety, Tim too had become a practitioner of doing what it took to survive. Nevertheless, he knew how far to go in allowing himself to become submerged. Whereas Little Man had no boundaries. Tim was also a straight A student in school, diligently dedicating himself to put priority on his education. Regardless of the strain the home environment placed upon him, he was determined to make something of himself and determined to escape the horrific presence of Dad.

There was a night-and-day difference between Tim and Little Man, providing for me two different mindsets towards life and its meaning. Each of them represented a model of some sort: one of them wild, carefree, and rebellious, while the other—though his temper was somewhat uncontrollable—desired to excel beyond the required years of schooling and contained a very positive outlook on life.

It appeared that Little Man had his sights set more on dodging dear ole Dad. He chose to associate with the neighborhood drunkards, thieves, gangbangers, and folks who obviously had no interest in school. By age fifteen, he had already concluded that school was a hindrance —"stopping me from enjoying life," he said.

Pushing his negative attributes aside, he was a prolific baseball player, left-handed, and Dad loved to watch him play. That was the one and only area of life they shared. He was amazing to watch, and, I could see that Little Man was possibly fulfilling a long hoped-for dream that Dad never had the opportunity of achieving (he had dropped out of school himself at a very early age for the sake of helping his family financially). He lived that part of his absent childhood through his son, as many parents attempt to accomplish, I only imagine.

My parents were sort of secretive when it came to speaking of their past. Neither of them shared any information in conversation pertaining to the history of their childhoods, nor did I ever hear from either of them about dreams entertained as a child. The closest I ever got to any of my grandparents was when we took summer vacations to Alabama and Mississippi, which I detested. But no sooner would we return from our supposed family vacation than the Twilight Zone resumed. The chaos was rebirthed. I could find no meaningful place amongst the ranting and raving. My own brothers and sisters misled me but not intentionally; they lived according to the way they knew how.

The older members were of age; they could hang out, go to parties, and indulge in activities I longed for. My earnest hope was to accompany each of them; on the other hand, I loved Mom too much to lay upon her any more burdens than what she was at present receiving. I knew she had been through a lot already, and something inside of me wanted to give her relief. She had suffered much, and although I couldn't fully understand at the time, she was already paying for her mistakes.

I admired Tim for his accomplishment, if truth be told; though he inadvertently came across as not wanting to have anything to do with me. Often, he gave me the impression that he couldn't have cared less if I was ever born. I was forced to turn my attention to Little Man solely in hope to gain some form of brotherly affection. That was an easy persuasion, actually. He was more than willing to spend as much time with me as one could ask, though what he had in mind was to teach me about the streets. How to shoot craps was the first lesson he wanted to teach me. Then how to roll up marijuana (weed); next was what drink of liquor would better give me the satisfaction of quenching my thirst. I thought that, as tempting as his invitation sounded, it would have to wait at least until I reached the age where I was no longer charged with chaperoning Mom to church. For now, I said, to myself, it would have to remain wishful thinking.

HOW MUCH CHURCH CAN ONE MAN TAKE?

THE all-day church event with Mom was too much for me to bear. At times the services lasted until late evening, and she was content to remain there until the very end of a seemingly endless occasion. I was frustrated from having to endure such theatrical renditions. In my book, those acts had no meaning. I no longer cared to watch the women perform a ritualistic dance that scared the daylights out of me. Often, their hats went flying in another direction, and even their wigs became detached. The entire scene to me was eerie; I wanted to leave as fast as I had arrived.

Apparently, to attend church with Mom wasn't enough because immediately after one of the exhaustive services sponsored by the man in the robe, Mom decided within herself that it would be a good idea if I joined. "Give your life to Jesus," she said. I didn't care to give my life to Jesus or to anyone else as far as I was concerned, but she insisted it was time. Taking me by the hand with a firm grip, she escorted me to the front where the man in the robe was standing. With everyone in the congregation watching me, he began asking me questions.

"Do you believe in Jesus? Do you believe that God raised Jesus from the grave? Do you believe that Jesus is the Son of God? Then, at the profession of your faith, you are saved."

I had no clue as to what he was saying. "Faith? What faith?" I asked myself. I had no faith. I only answered believing it was the right thing to do. I would have much preferred to be at home with Little Man.

I believed in God and as far as I was concerned, Jesus was God. Nevertheless, no one had ever clearly defined the difference between one or the other, their different roles for humanity. So, in response to the proposed questions asked, "Yes," was my reply. "Yes, yes, yes," was all I knew to say, believing from that point on t h a t I would undoubtedly be with God when I died.

Little did anyone know that the actual molding process was just beginning. Conspicuously I made my way through one of my sister's purses (I'm not sure which). Nonetheless, I stumbled across a stick of marijuana. I was no stranger to seeing it but had never experienced the effect it would have on me if I was   to smoke. I Extracted the pin joint from her purse as gently as a master surgeon performing his duties in the operating room. I knew what I was going to do with my discovered treasure. The next day of school, I would invite my good friend Richard to join me in my voyage to manhood. I knew he would hold no reservations in joining my experiment with the prize I found.

"Fire it up!" he said, excited that I had chosen him to be part of our rites-of-passage experiment. After all, where I came from, the way I was raised, drinking, partying, getting high, and "taking no mess" was the definitive makeup to manhood—or womanhood.

Richard and I shared many similarities. Like mine, neither of his parents were involved substantially in his progress with school. From what I knew, they never attended a parent conference in order to present even a remote display of concern. Although I didn't rank as anyone's favorite child in the community, little did they know that I did like making good grades. I liked school during this sixth-grade year. I was twelve years old and hoped for Mom and Dad to show some form of interest in my achievements.

Towards the end of my sixth-grade year, my attitude, I knew, was taking even more of a reckless turn. My temper was outrageous, and my once optimistic view of life began to grow dim. I felt that they didn't care how I was doing in school, and because of their neglect life became envisioned through negative eyes.

Geggy and I were still extremely tight, but gradually creeping into my midst was another category of peers I began to grow very fond of: the "gangbangers" and "Old Gangsters," or "OGs" for short. I liked what I saw about them, especially the pretty girls that flocked to them as if they were some sort of rock star. I made up my mind right then that as soon as I was of age, the people on the other side of the tracks would meet me!

I couldn't wait to grow up and leave the presence of Dad, yet the truth of the matter is that Dad offered no time for development, to come of age. It was duly noted by all what to expect once you reached age eighteen—your first-class eviction notice awaited you.

Mom had accomplished her mission of becoming an esteemed member of the women's auxiliary and usher board, doing much for the church of God. However, her busy schedule of providing tender, loving care (TLC) to the people outside of her immediate household would create problems. By devoting much of her time to self-recovery, the bonds of family that once kept us at least partially close would soon break all the more, Material items became her way of compensating Sharon and me for her absenteeism in our life.

There is no complaint; Sharon and I were spoiled rotten when it came to clothes, bicycles, and field trips with the school—and we loved it! Yet there were a few things, I believe, that both of us would have gladly traded our toys in for. I can't speak for Sharon, but my desire was to receive some one-on-one time; an occasional trip to my school, a question regarding how I was doing with my homework, and every now and then attend one of my karate practices.

Undoubtedly, the emotional neglect had its effects: insecurity, displacement, and obsessive materialism were the results. I had no identity of my own. I wasn't "confirmed," as they say, especially from Dad. Dad only emphasized that a man was "anyone who could hold down a full-time job and provide a roof over his family's head." Leaving me with that assumption, I figured nothing else was needed. Character was not an important asset to him, I guess. If so, it was never discussed. He believed passionately that as long as he fulfilled the golden rule of keeping a roof over our heads, his job was complete and an appreciation was due on his behalf.

Many days came that I longed to receive a "hello, son" as he entered the house from a hard day's work, but nothing came. I equally hoped to feel the pat of his huge hand grace my small back as an indication of a job well done. Likewise, nothing came. I wasn't important to him, I believed. I was excluded from all aspects of his life. I wasn't too young to search for something missing in my life, I told myself. Innocence was eluding me. And one thing I knew for sure was that if Dad didn't take me under his wing, surely those fellas at the other side of the neighborhood would.

I was fighting an emotional battle of confusion. I felt deprived of any intimacy with my parents. Some may say that men don't need intimacy—well, I disagree. Quickly I learned to find comfort in the material *things* they gave. The joy I looked for in a father was found in the presence of someone else's' old man or the OGs in the street.

It's been a long time coming

TIM'S proclamation on the importance of education was not in vain. I liked seeing the positive reaction on Mom's face when she saw the report card he'd bring home. I hoped to one day bring her that same joy. However, my passionate desire to do much of what I knew Little Man stood for was overwhelmingly equal. The contents of the world seemed impressive. The pleasures I perceived it offered from hearing Lanny and the others speak of with such enthusiasm was my ultimate destiny—at all costs.

I couldn't wait to accompany Little Man into the streets. Then again, I battled the notion of hurting Mom; I loved her a lot. Making her proud of me, just as she was of Tim, was a commitment in which I could in no way fall short. I remember the years when I sat at the base of her feet, rubbing her legs, hoping to extract the unwanted pain after one of her many fights with Dad.

The sixth grade did offer me more freedom and put an end to the once mandated obligation of chaperoning Mom to church. I was a big boy now, of age where I could finally see for myself what really took place on the other side of the tracks!

For Little Man, freedom had come several years prior; as for Tim, he was in his last year of high school, about to graduate. Soon he would be relinquishing his bed in Dad's house, leaving five of us to endure the contentious setting.

Envy rose to an all-time high due to the material possessions Mom always made sure that Sharon and I received. A few of my siblings felt as if they had never received the attention given to the two of us. Mom really had no idea that clothes and *things* weren't enough. Each new outfit only temporarily satisfied me. Sure, I appreciated being the best dressed child in the community, but, I needed more. I needed to know that I was cared for and loved through a manner other than with a toy. Emphatically, I sought to feel the loving arms from her embrace and her gentle, motherly stroke. I wanted to be heard, to have the right to speak freely about things that were possibly troubling me. I wanted the right to express to them whenever I didn't like something or felt scared for whatever reason or another. My words didn't matter, it seemed. "I'm the parent, and you're the child," to quote.

So, this is the "Other Side?"

FOR a long time, I dreamed of this environment, wondering if I would be able to keep up the pace. It was fast, and it seemed that everywhere I looked there were much older girls. They found me "attractive and cute," they said, and I welcomed their compliments. I thought Little Man would allow me to hang with him especially since I was a newcomer, yet he stated that I needed to involve myself with people my own age. That wasn't hard at all. Immediately I found acceptance and confirmation, some of which I desired from my parents. My evaluation of life was very shallow. Many times, I wondered why I was here in this world in the first place. What was my actual purpose? I knew that compassion ran deep inside me, but I couldn't assess how to present that side of me on a consistent basis.

I had deep compassion for people who had no place to sleep or any food to eat. And whenever we passed through the more impoverished communities, inside I wept just at the sight of little kids my age who were wearing clothes with holes in them or shoes that appeared very old. I didn't think that should be so. I hated that there were homeless people.

I always told Mom I would make a difference in this cruel world one day. I never figured that first I would have to undergo a grip from the world of new pleasures that, at present, projected a future contrary to what was embedded within the secret places of my heart. Despite my desires, my course was veering toward uncertainty. Nothing thrilled me more than to have finally reached an age where Mom believed that I was ready to be pardoned from attending church with her. Not that she let me off scot-free or anything; she just said that I was old enough to decide for myself where I wanted to attend. To honor her compromise, I attended a church located a short distance from where we lived and where my sister Gail, the one I presumed wicked, was also attending.

Mom was clueless as to my occasional drinking while under the supervision of Little Man. My goal was to keep it that way, in hopes of sustaining the untarnished image of being "Mommy's little baby boy." I loved the scenes that the other side displayed. The environment offered me pleasures that at will would set me free from the hurt, anger, and pain I felt inside. There was an enticement nudging you to take part in everything it had to offer. This was the phase of the Jekyll and Hyde syndrome, wanting to please Mom on one hand, yet sow my wild oats on the other. But, **"No man can serve two masters."**

Number Seven had become my identification tag from Mom. In fact, age seven is my first recount of hearing the biblical numerology. I had no idea of their numerical meanings and thought even less of their significance. She told me afterwards that seven was God's number and represented completion; three was   the number of the Trinity (I didn't know what the Trinity was, so that was useless information, I thought). She went on in more detail to explain that the Trinity represents the Father, who is God; the Son, who is Jesus; and the Holy Spirit—all of which make up the order of One God. "Oh, yeah, now I get it," I said to her, careful not to show from my facial expression that I was still bewildered. I did think about what she had said, pondering at times to myself, "Could what she said really be true?" Despite my endless feelings of present despair, a seed was planted. I began to wonder in more dept, the reason for my existence.

Dad and Little Man, though both growing older, were still like two rattlesnakes fighting for their survival. A midnight encounter erupted when Dad arrived home late from work one night, awakening my brother and me to go wash dishes that were left inside the kitchen sink. He insisted we "move at once or else!" His main focus was directed toward Little Man. Well, as usual, he once again received the short end of the stick. I could hear the verbal exchange from each of them as I sat at the top of the stairs, careful not to interrupt.

My normal tears were beginning to manifest from the anger I couldn't tame. I was fed up with what I had seen for far too long. My brother's pain I received as my own for many years. Idly I sat on the stairs, excusing myself from my still position only to make way for Mom as she passed by, headed to the scene where all the drama was taking place. She looked on helplessly and dismayed. Heartached, I would say, and even more fed up with everything.

"I'll wash them; just leave him alone." Although her murmur was a soft whisper, I could still hear her words. She was tired, I could only imagine. For many years, she had endured the contentious setting. I wanted to give her a break. "One day I will," I told myself. "One day, Mom'll be proud of me." I could never have allowed my extracurricular activities to become known; that would have killed her for sure, I thought. There I was, living a life of chaos outside the home, but in the presence of Mom … living another way. I was confused. I couldn't understand why the hunger for my father's approval weighed so heavily upon me, either. I didn't like him even the remotest. But even though I witnessed so much of his abuse and even still felt completely uncomfortable anywhere in his presence, I wanted his attention. There was something he had that I needed, I believed. What was I looking for?

I admired the fact that he was a devout provider. That is, the paying of bills, giving Mom money every week for groceries, and taking on the responsibility of raising four other kids besides his own. We never suffered financially; or at least, I didn't think we had it bad. Christmas was always the best day of the year for me, especially since my birthday was on Christmas Eve. I always received double of what anyone else received.

Junior high school would be beginning soon, and my first summer experience would come to an end. "It won't be my last!" I vowed to myself. The summer undoubtedly had its impact on me. It gave me the opportunity to experience first- hand new adventures and discoveries, like the night outings, the scenes with girls parading up and down the block. Everything was in place, it appeared!

The new group of fellas I chose to hang with were sticklers for having a good time. In fact, it was as if we were in violation of the law if we didn't drink every day. I wasn't much for the marijuana, but the smooth taste of Passion Punch wine coolers was another thing!

The summer also allowed me to see for myself the depth of what the street life really entailed. I got a bird's-eye view of the people who would inspire me. I looked on intently, studying the older Gs' behavior and, as we say, their "game." I was trying to see if I could pick up any tricks of the trade, so to speak. I really paid close attention to those who had been involved in the deep dynamics of the streets, considering them my best instructors. Although now, for whatever reason, they were reduced to living in alleyways or anywhere else they could find a suitable place to fall asleep. I told myself I would never be like they. "They are weak," I said. I had a hard time fathoming how a person could end up on the city streets devoid of life, jobless and homeless, especially after hearing their stories of once being in the military and some even going to college. Despite their current position, all of them still seemed to project an outward display as if they were completely content with the way their lives turned out.

My predeveloped thinking couldn't conceive that some were once productive people. Despite the distasteful observation of my surroundings, nothing registered that would deter me from my present course. I couldn't see, nor was I ever told, that things didn't happen overnight—they progressed. It was a firm fact in my mind that "this could never happen to me!"

My Early Morning Fix

THE day couldn't begin unless I hooked up with the crew. It was mandated that we get wasted before school began at 8:00 a.m. Some of the fellas had already entered high school, although they never went to class. Anyhow, it was "against creed," they said, for me to enter junior high school sober. I was soon to turn thirteen years old. And all we could think of was drinking, fighting, partying … life was a party! We thought, "Enjoy it now, you only live once!" None of us considered a plan for our future. There were unspoken plans that only I would share with myself. Nothing was openly expressed to the fellas. Inside me, despite my negative involvements, I was determined to make it through the seventh grade. In fact, I made up my mind that if I was to do nothing else in life I would graduate from high school.

But if I passed the seventh grade, I knew that it wouldn't come easily. I was struggling, never giving much thought that possibly the struggle was induced by my early morning devotions with Passion Punch Coolers. Math also contributed to my struggle; it was the subject I hated and struggled with whether I was high or sober. The drugs only increased my inability to focus. I didn't know that at first start. My beliefs were that the alcohol and drugs would heighten my senses and awareness. I was wrong.

The drugs performed the exact opposite of what I believed they would bring about. I couldn't focus; my attention span lasted no longer than a minute, and my assertiveness … well, I wasn't as sharp as I thought. But none of that mattered. All I was able to see was my present position, my here and now, my moments of pleasure. Nothing else was important, no grade, no teacher. For the brief moment of intoxication, all of my problems were gone.

My emerging identity was taking form at a rapid pace. All of the top name-brand clothing worn for any occasion, the freshly cut hair complemented by black curls, each injected a confidence I otherwise would not have had. The new image was tantalizing. I stayed fresh at all times, mimicking some of the OGs who confirmed that I was in good standing with the ghetto community. They defined me, effortlessly giving me a nickname that was sure to ring out in the neighborhood. It was the makeup of everything I presented from my external appearance that gave me my inward identity. If I wasn't wearing the right pair of pants or unable to obtain a haircut, then the person beneath the clothing remained the farthest from my knowledge.

Dad hadn't confirmed anything. There were no conversations about puberty, responsibility, money management, etc. But Mom had her share of the blame to receive as well, I often told myself. She was equally absent from my personal life, and that too contributed to my misguided attitude. The first year of junior high school wasn't bad. My focus was sometimes persuaded in the other direction; nonetheless, I made it through with fairly decent grades, I might add. I passed math with either a C or D average. I didn't care what I received as long as I passed.

My eighth-grade year consisted much of the same as did my seventh-grade year. The only difference was that the activities began to escalate. I was turning fourteen, and the lifestyle I was trying desperately to keep in balance began to take control of me. I couldn't see that at the time. As long as I was still attending some classes and making passing grades, I was okay. That's what I told myself, but too much pleasure is deceiving. All I wanted was to have fun! Before you know it, you're submerged, wondering how you ended up where you are. By the time you discover it, you're further entangled in its web.

They're off to a Great Start

I watched Mom and Dad bypass each other in the same manner week after week, with Dad yelling at the top of his lungs for Mom to tell him the whereabouts of his necktie. He wanted to know if the color he had chosen matched the rest of his outfit. Those mornings were amazing to watch, especially since Mom still had to dress Sharon. Things were better for the most part, but it was too late; I had been *molded*, shaped by the pleasures of sin and the OGs from the neighborhood. For the moment, surrendering my new life wasn't a consideration.

In the street life, success was measured by the type of car you drove, the kind of house you lived in, and the kind of clothes and feet gear you wore. But most importantly, you had to have a star female by your side with others waiting in the wings to fall back on just in case your primary didn't work out or made you upset, for whatever reasons. You had to have more than one female. There was no such thing as exclusivity. If you were really the man, you had a chick in every community. My objective was to have all of the above. But money outweighed everything. I was determined to travel the world and to live in a mansion, though not to forsake the unspoken desire in my heart kept secret from my gangbanging buddies. It was my secret that I had a passion to feed the hungry, help hurting kids, and do my part to make the world a better place.

However, no one told me that the million dollars I intended on having would come only through hard work, money management, careful planning, and most of all, patience.

At the time, I objected to any occupation that would take more than one year to achieve my goal. I thought, "Surely I'm not about to work for some white man with the power to dictate my future and pull the rug out from under me if he decided to close his business." Besides, they were the oppressors, I was told by the OGs. My goal was to be my own boss and have control over my own future. We all shared the common belief that money made happiness, and if there was no money, then there could be no happiness. "Money was the key to happiness!"

Constantly, I heard complaints from both my parents about the lack of money and amount of bills. Honestly, I thought we were financially stable, a lot better off than many of my peers. They would say how exhausted they were from working so hard and bringing home so little money to show for it. Little did they know how their open display of dread prompted me to look upon the entire thought of becoming an adult with disgust and fear. I wanted no part of embarking upon that road of life, especially, if what appeared before me was the way it would be when I became a man. I was determined never to have money problems. I could have many other problems, but money, I would get it by any means necessary!

A Promise Kept

I kept my promise to Mom, still attending the church of my choosing. I knew that was the one thing I could do that would please her. This time, I invited James, an older guy who had become a good friend. I asked him if he was up for doing something different. Without even knowing the details, he gave no resistance. Once hearing my suggestion to attend church with me, he expressed even more enthusiasm. He knew, just as I knew, that there were a lot of beautiful young girls who also attended. "Church wouldn't be too bad," we said to each other, all the while, promoting a scheme that would allow us to get in good with the girls of our choice.

This church was lively, much livelier than the church I attended with Mom. It was better structured, and the singing was better, as well. But the best part of it all? There wasn't a bunch of elderly women blocking my view with their big hats.

It Only Takes A Seed

THIS particular minister was different, as well. To me he got his point across, meaning that even I could understand that if I didn't have Jesus—"truly have Jesus"— then hell and its angels awaited me. That scared the heck out of me, and since James later reiterated the pastor's sermon, it was obvious he too felt uneasy about the message. There definitely was an indescribable seed deposited in both of us at that moment. Even if there was no visible evidence of change, something was inserted. This I knew for sure.

That wasn't the first time I heard a minister speak of how Jesus could turn your life around. "Change it for the better if you just allow Him," was one minister's exact quote in the past. Those words at the time had no relative meaning, so I dismissed them and concluded there was nothing wrong with my life; however, this time was different. I actually listened to what he had to say. Although at times I was unable to control my eyes from glancing around the sanctuary, scoping to see who would become my prey. The girls were the main reason I agreed to go in the first place, I told myself. Well, two reasons—Mom. I loved her.

Fourteen years of age and I still didn't care to be anywhere in Dad's presence; I fled the house at every chance. His bad aura continued to be too much. To me, he was still unapproachable. Or possibly I was branded too deep from my childhood and just prejudged him, overlooking if even he had made the slightest change (had I given him a chance?). At any rate, whenever I wanted something, I went by way of Mom.

One day, out and about, looking for some action, one of my homies pulled a small packet from his pocket. It was aluminum foil. After sharing what it was, he made his rounds, nudging everyone to taste. I was down for anything; therefore, sampling the powder cocaine was just another day's event. I wasn't impressed. It wasn't what I had heard it would be.

Or maybe I didn't know what to look for regarding the feeling it was supposed to bring. Alcohol was my strongest desire at the time—Passion Punch Coolers! Cocaine, it did nothing for me. I was convinced the road I was traveling had become irreversible. I heard Little Man clearly say that it was much too late for any reconciliation between him and Dad. He felt he was old enough now to express explicitly how he felt about the massive abuse inflicted upon him as a child. He did just that, as if he waited his entire life for that moment. He stated that his abuse was unmerited, that he was abused for absolutely no reason at all and would *never* forgive the man who did that to him. He found more love in the streets, he shared with me, and as much as I wanted to disagree with his claim, I was unable.

The crap games, bar parties, and now sex added into the equation heightened the addiction to the concrete, jungle world. Everything associated with the street life pleased me. I watched the OGs sit on a broken wall in an alley, passing around the forty-ounce bottle of Old English 800, never wiping the tip of the bottle. "The man's beer," they called it.

All of their discussions escalated into a competition of war stories. Most of them were lies, by the way, and they knew that the story they shared was a lie. But that wasn't the point behind telling it. No, it was to gain a better status and street fame.

Everything I witnessed as a child, along with the partial hatred I still harbored inside towards Dad made obedience to authority difficult. I admit, there was no discipline. My rebellious attitude only served its purpose around those of like minds. I was accustomed only to hearing words spoken in the form of a command. Dad also made it a point to identify each male child descriptively by the plantation word *boy*. At first, hearing it so much made you rethink if your name was really what you heard others call you. I hated that word.

I wanted to use my pellet gun to do to him as I had done to the little robins that sat in the tree located in my backyard. POP! Was the sound I heard from my pellet gun as I watched the bird fall to the ground. In order to complete the mission, I had to rush over to implant another pellet into the little birds head, just in case the first shot failed to accomplish my intended purpose—to kill. For an instant, Dad had become my next robin.

My negative behavior was snowballing. The participation in fighting, smoking, drinking, and hiking to one of our neighbor- hood department stores in order to steal the latest addition of Tyco cars carried us full speed down a path that would clearly hinder our course for a productive lifestyle. We never assessed the final consequences of our actions; all we knew was that for the brief moment in our lives, life was worth living!

Most of our theft derived from boredom. None of us were poor; just the thrill of seeing if we could get away with the items gave us a rush. My grades weren't the greatest and there was no possible chance of my making anyone's honor roll, but they were sufficient in order for me to pass onto the ninth grade.

Church on Sundays took us away from our catastrophic lifestyle, proving to be a good thing for us if only in a small measure. We appreciated the new atmosphere. It gave us a break from our destructive course (sometimes, you need a break). The senior church members who were proud of our commitment extended the invitation for us to join the church choir. That came as a shock.

We considered their proposal carefully, mainly concentrating on the fact that the choir membership would give us privileges. The privileges were important, but our primary objective, I say again, was solely to gain the respect of some gorgeous females with whom we wanted to become better acquainted.

During one of our choir rehearsal days, the girls discovered our secret of attending rehearsal intoxicated or high. That didn't go over very well with them. Vehemently they preached nonstop of how wrong it was to drink and use drugs … "especially while singing in the choir." We didn't see anything wrong with it; after all, we were going to church like everyone said we should. "Besides," we replied, "we accepted Jesus as our Lord and Savior" (*Lord* had an entirely different meaning, I'd come to learn. But at the time, He was Lord and Savior.)

Meanwhile, we brushed aside their interjections of moral, biblical standards and strolled in the direction of our clubhouse,

an abandoned two-family house. As we walked steadily to our own sanctuary, they continued to shout that we were committing an abominable act against God.

We were convinced that their sole purpose for being in our presence that day was to dissuade and bring conviction to our souls, but we weren't buying it. "This is our time; Jesus has his on Sundays," we jokingly retorted. The girls appeared to have our best interest, but their timing was wrong. The last thing we wanted was to hear the Ten Commandments preached by some stuffy church girls. In just a few minutes, the medication that allowed each of us to express our truest feelings was about to be injected, and there were to be no outside interruptions. "It's our life, and we have the right to live it any way we see fit," we said from a distance and agreeing in unison. We enjoyed their company but could have done without being told how we ought to live our lives. We felt their comments really gave us a reason to crack the lid of the forty-ounce Old-English 800 and Budweiser beer. "Let's start our own personal church service," we said in laughter as we entered the abandoned building.

Neither James, nor I possessed any passion for church; it was simply another form of extracurricular activity. Even though we liked the atmosphere and occasionally the pastor would say something relevant, we gained nothing that would definitively seal our faith and cause us to abandon the lifestyle we had become so accustomed to living. We had no full knowledge of how or why we were actually serving the Lord in the first place. All we received were "Band-Aid remedies." Without understanding, how could we follow? While in contrast, the clubhouse gave us a place to retreat, hide out from the police, and a place to just "chill out" whenever we no longer cared to go within the confines of our individual homes, for whatever reason. Then, as soon as we were properly medicated, nothing this evil world hurled our way would be too difficult for us to handle, we all believed.

The days passed rather quickly, going from one day watching Mom and Dad reaching for each other's jugular veins to within a few weeks—high-school!

HIGH SCHOOL TRIALS

I was losing interest in school all together. When school was important to me, my parents showed absolutely no interest. I was far from being a stupid kid and had absolutely no learning disability. In fact, I was quite intelligent; however, the riotous living gripped me in a way unexplainable.

Mom saw that my behavior was progressing from bad to worse. She often emphasized that I should terminate my relationship with James, B, Larry, Chuck and the other "juvenile delinquents. If you was smart, you would spend more time with someone like Geggy," she added. I really didn't appreciate her statement. "Why don't you stop trying to choose my friends?" I lashed back at her in my defense.

Her point wasn't that Geggy didn't do anything wrong, that he was this perfect little angel. No, just that she knew he came from a family of peers who wanted something out of life, who had a value system. Even if they did indulge in drinking, she was sure there were no drugs amongst them, and everyone was committed to graduating from high school.

"So, this is high-school!" I said. Entering the huge building for the first time was an organic experience. The corridors were three times the size of the hallways in my junior high school. The number of people made me feel as if I were a little fish in a big pond.

People were congested in every area of the building, talking about only God knows what. It seemed to be a very long wait to get here, but here I was—high school! Withrow High School, the place where all my brothers and sisters attended. And for those fortunate enough to have graduated, a place where the school's *alma mater* would forever be endearing to their heart.

I made a point to attend all of my assigned classes for the first week. I wanted to at least get a feel for the teacher and the required subject. The importance of school was quickly going in the opposite direction. Truthfully, I just wasn't that interested anymore. The joys of new freedom and excitement began to override the once held desire to do well. "This was just too much fun!" I told myself. Besides, as time went on the frustration I developed towards my so-called "history education" class was repulsive.

It was frustrating having to sit inside a boring classroom for forty-five minutes. "For what?" I asked myself, "Only to learn about someone else's history?" From my point of view, or from the excluded information the teacher just happened to leave out, Blacks had no history, were unworthy of recognition, or hadn't contributed anything to this country. At any rate, the failure to teach me anything to which I could relate infuriated me.

Little Man was as good as gone from school already. If by chance he would have remained in school, this would have been his senior year. Mentally, he had retired his membership long ago; now he was simply going through the motions. He was still on the enrollment sheet, but his presence located anywhere other than the hallways or the outside campus could be forgotten.

I followed his pattern of "dating the halls" for a good while. We often hid in restrooms until the hall monitors ended their walkthrough to ensure there were no stragglers still around. We always dodged them. We had our own little perfect hideaway. Then, as soon as the coast was clear, each of us who carried our steel gadgets, exclusively designed for cracking locks, quickly began our rampage through lockers to see if we could "ante-up" the after-school liquor money.

Our number one purpose was to provide a clear expression of how the world looked from our perspective. We were determined to make it obvious to everyone that there were misery and unhappiness stored in each of us. The only rules we were willing to follow, we told ourselves, were our own. We believed the only laws that applied to us—which were forbidden to break—were the laws of the streets. There was a code of ethics the OGs always said to follow.

Too Much Freedom

IT was common practice for us to do the things we were doing: breaking and entering, stealing from department stores, pursuing females, drinking, smoking, and everything attached to being a member of the street life. Then, when that particular day was over, you were obligated to make a commitment to meet tomorrow for a reenactment of today's activities.

I was fifteen, turning sixteen soon and the additional freedom I gained from Mom and Dad was overwhelming. My favorite adventure was to go roller skating. I began to accompany some of the other kids in an all-night skating session. This session lasted from 8:00 p.m. until 6:00 a.m.! This was the icing on the cake. No matter how much I appreciated the extra liberty, there were times I wanted to be told to return by a specific hour. That would have given me some indication they cared, I thought. Mom really did care, I believed with all my heart, but to let me have my way all the time ... I really didn't want that. Some parents believe giving a child everything they want, when they want it, is the truest demonstration of love. But the Bible says that, "The Lord chastises those He loves." Sometimes, "NO!" is a demonstration of love.

It was time for my first-quarter report card which I really had no desire to see. "WOW," I said, "what a mess." I knew I couldn't allow Mom to see it. Not out of fear, but out of love. Even if she wanted to see it, there was no way I was going to allow that to happen. Convincing her that we hadn't received our report cards was simple. She never attended anything or even inquired regarding my progress, so it was nothing for me to give her misleading information. As far as she knew, I was an A or B student.

Before I knew it, I was well into my fourth quarter; and thus far, with the exception of biology, I remained at a C average. Even math, my most hated subject, I passed with a C or D average. Every subject except English was a complete waste of my time, I thought. Nevertheless, a spirit inside of me continued to thrust me in a forward movement. Even when I had no intentions of going to class, I was pushed to excel beyond my own misguided desires. The echo of Mom's voice never left me, either. Her emphasis on the number seven, for some reason, continued to pop up in my head at the most inopportune times, even during my drinking moments. "To please Mom," repeated my unconscious voice that became impossible for me to shake. Her change was also admirable; even if I hadn't received the kind of affection t h a t I desired to receive from her, something gave me confirmation that she really did love me. That motivated me, little did she know. And despite my outward display of incorrigibility, my inward man was willing to give it everything he could.

The most important thing Mom desired of me and all of her children was to attend church. The grades were an important factor, but church took precedence. She was proud of my contribution to the choir; it showed each time we spoke of the new songs I learned. It would have killed her if she knew I was drunk and high upon rehearsals. I enjoyed the church life and truly believed I would always have it included in on my list of things to do.

She stated how God honors "faithfulness and dedication." Well, not being an adamant Bible reader, I was clueless as to what she meant. At any rate, she was proud, and a smile was upon her face; therefore, I was content. Although at times, I wondered if underneath all of her smiles and humming there was any real happiness inside. After all, her family was still in shambles.

I found many stories mentioned in the Bible hard to believe. For instance, the verse that spoke of Jesus feeding 5,000 people with two fish and five loaves of bread, or the story of Peter walking on water. The minister preached a sermon about going to hell, and that it's only by faith in which you can stand against the devil; that, I had no trouble receiving. I heard Mom mention faith quite often, though U never understood its definition. "Faith and obedience," she said repeatedly.

One day I made a special effort to search meticulously for any reference similar to the preacher's sermon. For the second time he had said something that induced fear inside of me. I feared the thought of going to hell, especially for eternity. I feared dying, if truth was to be told, but hell was completely out of the question. But there were other principles I was taught that had created a stone wall, prohibiting anything that would permit a change to take place right away.

I revisited the dream of becoming someone great in life, remembering when I told Mom that I was going to make a change in the world and how I would make people feel better about themselves. Believe it or not, I wanted to see people happy even more than I wanted money. However, I didn't think that was possible because of my old philosophy: it was money that made happiness. My ambition had not diminished, and despite the fact that my grades were at the bottom of my class it didn't stop me from dreaming.

Sure, there were times when skepticism appeared but only out of lack of knowledge, from not knowing how exactly I was going to turn my dream into my reality. Moreover, who would help me in my quest? It was not obvious to anyone who observed me from the outside that I even wanted to do something with my life besides drink, get high, and chase females. My outward demonstration implied to the judgmental onlookers that I was useless and wouldn't amount to anything. They were accustomed to witnessing some of our drunken celebrations and were convinced that we were all traveling down a dead-end road.

"I hate those fake, Christian want-to-be, holier-than-thou people; they are always judging someone." I said to James in frustration. The looks they gave us were excruciating. Not once did they encourage us. Some never even invited us to attend church with them, yet they passed judgment without giving it a second thought.

The inward tug of war intensified. The war signified itself as some form of conscience, or best said, spiritual awakening. The fact remained that Little Man and the daily rituals sponsored by the "thugs" who poured out a thimble full of liquor from their beer cans or bottles before taking a sip as a symbolic gesture for the homies who were either dead or in jail provided no conceptual, positive image. But these were my role models, my encouragers, the only people I knew for sure who would listen to whatever I had to say. This was becoming my comfort zone, and the people around me—my family. If there was any innocence left inside of me, it was gradually slipping away. I wanted to graduate, and that I would do. But the evil I harbored inside would take much more work to eliminate.

The cycle of drinking continued, progressing unknowingly, to say the least. By now, the power to abolish the stronghold had become too great. The OGs were clutching me, molding me slowly into their image. Dad had dissed me long enough, I told myself. Because of my resentment towards him, I was allowing every deceptive, artificial image of manhood to take the place of what he alone should have taught me.

Church played its role in depositing something of an alternative course, I suppose, but *it wasn't my time.* The superficial image of manhood presented by the OGs appeared definitive. In my mind, everything a man was supposed to be was right before my face; Jesus was nothing more than a gateway into heaven. All I had to do was *believe.*

Everything I observed from my surroundings, either positive or negative, became my makeup. Many people at school seemed to possess something I wanted, some sort of characteristic or self-projection of who they were. Whereas I still was on a mission of self-discovery. "Who am I?" I often wondered. I knew who they said I was, but any image I could possibly imitate inside the home was misleading. There was a deep void, I felt, and something needed to fill the emptiness quickly. As a chameleon, I absorbed bits and pieces of anyone I presumed could offer me an exclusive understanding of the questions I had in my mind.

The liquor sometimes made me revisit the years when Mom and Dad were fighting. I don't know why that was the case. It seemed the more I drank, the angrier I became. The liquor also made me recount the times when a white police officer shot and killed a young black kid in my neighborhood, with no one having to answer for what they had done.

I guess I was just an angry kid, because, each time I thought of not learning something in reference to black history from my history education teacher, I grew angrier—certainly after watching the old movies displaying how white folks hung and beat my black ancestors, not to mention the harassment we received from little white boys who called us "nigger" whenever we passed through their neighborhood. I hated this evil world, and white people were at the top of my hate list. Only the medication could help my fragmented emotions, I thought. I asked James, first thing in the morning before we'd even get off his front porch, "What are we drinking today?"

I knew I hadn't done very well. So, I figured it wouldn't matter if I closed the rest of the school year out with a bang! My only desire was to pass, which I did, all except biology.

Time is Moving On

THE same struggle I encountered during my ninth-grade year was also true for the tenth. "Time is moving on," I told myself. I began to notice that at the turn of each new age my innocence eluded me all the more. I considered that soon I'll be eighteen; "in two years, in fact," I told myself, then Dad'll be looking me in my eyes, asking to hear of my future plans." Regardless of my *desire,* my ability to lead a life consistent with my desire was unable to merge so that I could turn my desire into reality. Fact was, we were growing older and it was time to start planning towards our future.

I was sixteen now, soon to be seventeen, and knew that Dad meant every word he spoke in the past regarding his proclamation to evict. I wasn't about to leave my future to chance. I knew it was time to buckle up and take school more seriously if I wanted to graduate. I made huge improvement concerning my grades. The once C or D average had turned into a B, and in some classes I even managed to obtain an A. I was proud of myself. The productive track of life I desired to ride on was finally beginning to take me to my destination! So I thought. I counted my eleventh-grade year as an awakening. Nothing had changed concerning my running buddies. The only thing different was my determination to do something that would not only please Mom but also me!

I was determined not to follow the pattern of dropping out of school, as Little Man had done. Whereas he at least once showed up to walk the halls, eventually that was no longer a part of his agenda. He demonstrated with clear conscience that school was a waste of his time, and when he reached the age where he could terminate himself from entry, school became an embroidered memory. The streets proceeded as his biblical paradise. Apparently, he found comfort inside the chaos. Appearing somewhat defeated from the actual world's day to day events. I believed his new environment helped play a significant role in causing him to relinquish his hopes and dreams. He was completely gifted, and I would have loved to see him function in the area he displayed so well, to play baseball.

There was no doubt that my course was set in stone to repeat the model in front of me if I didn't quickly receive a divine eye opening. School had improved, but my wild indulgences still ranked at the top of my everyday duties. I saw myself living in the mansion and driving the fancy car. But life— this life I was engulfed in—held me as a hostage. Its grip was relentless in its efforts to keep me and anyone else caught in its clutches from ever escaping. How could I have ever imagined that it would grow worse before it grew better?

The visual should have been enough to make me redirect my course. Instead, blinded by insidious activities, I could only see the pleasure it gave, not the pain. I kept up a good front, but the heaviness from desire and the hatred of this world was too much for me to handle. Unhappiness made its way inside, cultivating the emptiness from wanting to grasp anything to fill the void. It wasn't solely about the girls anymore. I wanted the emptiness to go away. I grew in tune with the minister's message. Or possibly it was that I was growing tired of the life I was living. In any case, his words had some relevance to them; he was relating to my life. Speaking of more than just a heaven or hell, he spoke of real-life scenarios, things I never had explained to me. What he said made a lot of sense: "I did need some direction in my life," I thought, agreeing with his message.

He passionately conveyed that one needed to have a personal relationship with Jesus. I heard that particular statement preached before, I remembered, though it was many years ago.

I knew things were different inside of me. Regardless of the fact that I still made a beeline to the clubhouse to engage in a drink fest with the fellas, some changes were happening inside of me. I knew it because to be in a classroom passing with honor-roll status was something even I had trouble believing. But the road ahead still dealt me unimaginable obstacles.

THE GAME IS CHANGED

I had developed a new running buddy named Mike. We hung like two brothers, or should I say connected twins; when you saw one, you saw the other. I was proud to cruise us in my spotted Maverick car that Tim had given me. It was 1985, going into 1986. This was my senior year of high school. I made it! Through all the obstacles and heartaches, I never failed. It was the year of breakdancing when rap had first hit the scene. The year of LL Cool J, Slick Rick and Doug E. Fresh, Kurtis Blow and Run-DMC had hit the rap industry hard. The year when Mike and I were addicted to reciting the words of Slick Rick and Doug E. Fresh, jumping in on key whenever the part saying "word Rick" came across. However, he always replaced *Rick* with *D*, and I, returning the "word," never broke stride to the original lyrics. When the pool parties at Stuart Park were explosive, everyone from every community it seemed came to our neighborhood to party. That year some wannabe thug tried to diss us and take us for being weak; he had the nerve to make threats to us because he thought we were gaming on his girl. We were, but he didn't know that for sure.

"I had enough of his lip service, Mike; stay right here," I said, jumping into the Maverick. My thoughts were already on going to the house to retrieve my dad's hunting rifle. I wanted to put a couple of slugs in him. My parents were away on vacation in Alabama and Mississippi. I ran into the house. Before grabbing it to leave, I checked to see if there were any bullets inside. Happy with my observations, I carefully laid the rifle onto the backseat of the car and hurried back to the scene to handle my business. When I arrived, he was gone. I wonder if I would have shot him.

Thus far, I had kept my promise to make it, at least to this point. Accomplishing my goal of making it through the eleventh grade had been achieved. As discussions came by way of my guidance counselor it was understood that in order for me to graduate, I would have to make up a ninth-grade biology course in summer school, also stating that, "It would be in your best interest to enter a work program; the extra credit would give you the required number of credits." I had no problem with her recommendation. If graduating was contingent upon summer school, then summer school it was going to be. I didn't think twice about my decision.

Mike had transferred from another school and since I was in good standing with the teacher, I maneuvered to have him placed into the work program with me. The work was a cinch. Actually, I found it to be below the academic standards to which I was accustomed; thus, it took little effort to pass. In fact, I made honor roll for the first time ever, and was honored as classroom president—whatever that meant. Nonetheless, it was a great honor to, for once in my life, experience the feeling of honor status!

This arrangement had its perks like none other. The teacher permitted us to drink sodas in the classroom. That was just what we needed in order to smuggle in our liquor. We met in the restroom every morning, which we converted into our own personal boardroom. Dan, a guy who shared the same birthday as I, was responsible for bringing the gallon of Old Crow liquor; Mike, my running buddy, brought the Bacardi Dark. Since I only drank liquor with a light color to it, it was understandable that I'd bring Barcardi Light. I also brought the marijuana since I was the only person who maintained a weed connection. We poured the mixtures of liquor into our soda cans. The teacher never realized that inside of them was our "soothe juice." This will keep us in perfect harmony, we told ourselves, laughing.

Inside the classroom, I often kept a book standing in the upright position. This was to block the teacher's view while I twisted up a mountain of joints for Mike and me to sell to the weedheads. Mike sat next to me, acting as my lookout man. As soon as I finished twisting enough joints for the anxious customers, I turned my full attention once again to the teacher, just as a good little student should. This particular program required that in order to graduate, you had to find a job. The job served as graduating credits. You were only required to attend school for half the day, while the other half of the day consisted of work. You could even use half the day to go and fill out applications. I took full advantage of this program. Mom, knowing the criteria of the program, confronted me one evening after school. She told me she had a friend who worked for a life insurance company and suggested that I go the next day to fill out an application. She stressed that I use her as a reference.

MY FIRST REAL JOB

THE building of the life insurance company was as big as my high school. "Wow!" I said, "What can I possibly do in there?" Upon entering the front area, I immediately noticed the sign that read *Customer Service*. I glanced around to get a better view of the atmosphere. Out of nowhere, the receptionist interrupted me. "May I have an application?" I asked, "and if it's not too much trouble, may I please speak with Jim?" I did as Mom requested. Also, I had the opportunity to fill out the application while there on site. Immediately I received an interview. The interviewer stated that I should hear something within a week. "If you don't hear from me in a week, call me."

"Yes, sir," I said.

Within a week, just like the bald-headed man had said, I was called to begin work as a dishwasher. My first real job! Mom saw that I also was maintaining a good work record. She was proud and often stated for me to "keep up the good work." I still harbored fears inside. It didn't matter that I was eighteen now, my legal age for becoming dad's evictee. There was still no idea of what I wanted to do concerning my life. College was definitely a consideration, but would they pay the tuition?

I reflected on how I partied my way through my first, second and some of my third year of high school; now, as a senior, I participated in our lunchtime reunions held in the stadium before I separated and headed for my new job. I was a part of the working world, and it felt good! As the preacher had asked, "How long will you bathe yourself in the pleasures?" To me, my indulgence was only recreational. I failed to believe that the OGs sleeping in the alleyways could ever be me. My youthful ignorance devalued the meaning of progression. Therefore, unknowingly, every sip of liquor I took and every toot of powder cocaine

I began to sniff actively before work produced another seed towards addiction, making the chances of imitating those whom I swore never to imitate a possible reality.

Graduation was quickly coming upon us and another chapter in my life soon to close. Yet the echoes of Dad's words still rang in the back of my mind. His harsh proclamation of being "put out" awakened. There were decisions that needed to be made quickly on my part, decisions pertaining to what I was going to do with my life after I graduated. Tim was my motivation to go forward. College was a thought I entertained. I hated Ohio; there was no denying it, and I wanted desperately to leave this miserable, racist place. I wrestled continually with my emotions. Cincinnati, in my opinion, was an infested, overly racial, conservative city where any color other than white stood little chance of ever becoming a significant figurehead.

Mission Accomplished

APPROXIMATELY a few weeks, and graduation rehearsals would begin! I worked hard to make it this far, I acknowledged to myself. *And even if I wasn't in the top of my class, I made it through,* rendering my own pat on the back. If going to college didn't pan out, then the United States Army would be my alternative plan, I stated to a friend. I hadn't forgotten about summer school; nothing could be accomplished without the completion of my ninth-grade biology course. "I'm ready!" I told myself.

Graduation rehearsal was a blast! I'm sure my excitement mainly came from the fact that at each rehearsal I was inebriated. The smell of alcohol reeked through my pores, so much so that the music teacher, Mrs. Mannes, demanded that I sit in the rear. She stated how she didn't want my liquor odor to affect anyone else. Due to my overindulgence, my acute hearing failed me. I was certain I heard the announcement to eject our graduation caps into the air. But as certain as I was, I noticed my cap was the only hat sailing precariously upward. I didn't perceive this at the time, but there was a symbolic attachment to the display. A sort of *déjà vu* designed to give me a glimpse of the journey my life would ultimately take. A vision of some sort interrupted as I watched the hat hit the auditorium floor. At the time, I never connected that possibly God was showing me that destruction, pain, despair, heartache, loneliness, trepidation, and death were in my future.

Never would I see this part of my life again, I thought to myself. It was the final day before graduation and I knew I was blessed to have made it this far. If it was left up to me and my feelings, I would have abandoned school a long time ago. But the man inside of me just wouldn't let me quit.

It was June 1986, the day I worked extremely hard to encounter. Both

Mom and Dad were there to watch the momentous occasion. Afterwards, Mom offered to surrender the car as a token of her gratitude, but my father, interjecting into the conversation, disagreed. He didn't care that I had just completed twelve struggling years of school, nor the obstacles I had to climb. This should have been the one day of my life where he could have demonstrated his love for me. Instead, his callous, unaffectionate, selfish personality of old gave indication that he was still the same ole Dad, and I was furious.

"The day of my graduation, and he won't even let me use the car!" I was madder than I had ever been before. "All of the other fathers allowed their sons to drive wherever the after-party would be held, but mine … !" My thoughts wouldn't release me, and the feelings I felt towards him when I was a child resurfaced even more. "This is my special day and what do I get?" Left sitting on a brick wall to smoke weed, sniff a line of cocaine, and drink Old English 800!" I hated him for that. I felt he was as low down as any human being can be. I did what I knew to do, which was to grab Mike, James, and the rest of the crew to create our own party! We were about to wreak havoc in the community!

An Easy "A"

S UMMER school was a breeze. I passed the biology course with an A. Mom was confident I had turned my life around. She wanted to know what kind of plans I had come up with, if any. She knew that Dad was going to evict me, and I guess she just wanted to feel good in knowing that I had made some plans. I had spoken previously to some Army and Air Force recruiters in reference to entering the military. It was not something I wholeheartedly wanted to do, but my options were very limited.

Dad had long ago stated that he wouldn't pay the tuition for me to attend college, and in my ignorance, I knew nothing about financial aid or any other program that could assist me. I was caught in a dilemma again. One part of me desperately wanted to disappear from any presence of Dad, yet the other part of me wanted to enroll in the University of Cincinnati or even a community college.

That summer I made my decision to take the Army's entry examination, thinking of my brother Tim when I made the reservation. He entered the Air Force several years after high school. He had put in a couple years of college in Ohio. I admired him for his accomplishments, and now it was my time. There were urgent decisions needed to be made, and if I didn't inform Dad of my plans, he would make them for me, I was sure.

The Army Reserves, First

IT was settled. The United States Army it would be, but only on reserve status. These were my initial plans. I thought I could enter the reserves; in turn, it would provide a way to pay for my college tuition. My plan was to kill two birds with one stone, so to speak.

My employers at the life insurance company had no reservations pertaining to my decision. They mentioned that, after my initial training was complete, my job would be waiting for me upon return. It was all mapped out! I saw my life headed in the direction I had always dreamed! The only thing standing in my way was the Army proficiency test.

I sat in the crowded room with at least fifty others who had the same idea. The sweat rolled through my palms. My nerves fluttered uncontrollably for fear of failing the test. At least, that's what I told myself. But in reality, I knew it was from the possibility of an awaited eviction notice. My focus was dreadfully impaired. In addition, I heard of the war stories regarding boot camp from some of the vets in the neighborhood. "How could I believe anything from them, the *barrio* winos?" I asked, myself. I believe their plan was to scare me, a little game they liked to play with the younger Gs. Whatever the case, the fear wouldn't leave.

After I was done testing, I sensed that I had done poorly. It wasn't because of stupidity, but lack of concentration, I knew. I assured myself that I would retest if I was to fail and vowed that if that were the case, no matter what, the next time I would pass with flying colors.

I held on to my job at the life insurance company as a dishwasher. I liked it and knew that I needed to have some form of income. I wasn't a child anymore, and Dad was about to hold me accountable to my share of the rent. A dishwasher definitely wasn't my future career choice. I studied much harder, the part of the test I had failed. My desire to leave Cincinnati grew even more intense. I wanted to embrace something new, I said to myself. I wanted to break free from my negative surroundings. Things were growing old for me. The drinking, partying, and all-out same routine, I couldn't withstand anymore. In essence, I guess, I was ready for a change.

I'll Try Again

THE news I anticipated finally came. "Yes, this is he," I said, answering the telephone. "Mr. Smith," he said, "Sorry to inform you, sir, but you did not pass the test this time; however, if you choose to do so, you are welcome to retest after thirty days." "I'd be glad to, sir." I replied. I was confident this time I would pass. My strategy was to free my mind from fear of failure and of Dad. I was discouraged by the news that I had failed the test, but I knew that if I studied, the results would be different. "In thirty days, I'll retest, and pass!" I told myself.

It was the same atmosphere as before. There were a lot of people waiting to take the test for the first time, and some, I suppose, there to retest just as I was. It took many hours, but this time I sensed I had done much better. I left the testing station with confidence, unlike before when I had left in dread.

The wait to hear from the recruiter seemed longer than before. Apparently, the recruiter didn't know that I was on borrowed time. Dad was growing antsy. I was legally an adult now, according to the law: eighteen years of age, a man. However, I wasn't a man. In fact, I was very much so a child. The same child who covered his ears at each screeching sound of pain that pierced the air of his home, the same child that looked to his Mom and Dad for protection and hopes of receiving some form of tangible evidence of their love, and very much the child who wished for his dad to be present on the sideline during one of his baseball games or karate practices to cheer him on. Instead, I created my own path and made my own decisions. And now, it was up to me to discover my own place in this big world, all alone.

I ran out of patience waiting for the Army recruiter to call. My first instinct was to round up James and head for the recruiter's office just a few miles from my home. We reached the office in record speed. "I want to know," I said to James. "I need to know!"

This was the moment of truth, I told myself, determined that if I failed the test a second time, then it was fate telling me that the military was not my course.

I entered the office hoping to locate the recruiter who had handled my primary enlistment. I introduced myself to the first person in an Army uniform, with confidence, as always. It was a heavy-set man who sat behind the steel desk. I informed him as to my reason for coming. After listening, he motioned for me to have a seat in one of the chairs by the wall. In a most courteous tone of voice, he stated that he was going to the back to retrieve my test scores. The recruiter who primarily handled my case wasn't there at the time, I suppose; therefore, he took it upon himself to assist me. Returning rather quickly and holding in his right hand a folder with my name on it, he began to express his concerns in certain areas of testing. He further went on to say that he believed I could do much better. I didn't care to hear that nonsense, I just wanted to know if I passed, I said to myself. After completing his ritual, he closed with, "Nonetheless, you passed!" This was the best news I had heard in a very long time (except the news that I could graduate).

I was anxiously rushing to get home to share the good news with Mom and Dad. All I could think of from that point on was that I was about to travel, see the world, and meet new people. "I'm about to live!" I said, rejoicing. This was really a time for celebration, I thought. James and Mike both understood that if I wanted to drink, I best do it now for in a few weeks, my drinking will all be over until after boot camp.

Everyone was excited to hear the news! Mom received relief just from knowing that I was getting away from my bad influential homies; she never failed to emphasize that "none of them wanted anything out of life, anyhow. If they stay on the road they're on, they're all headed for destruction." She stated that they were all stranglers of my dreams and hindering me from accomplishing God's purpose for my life. She further mentioned that "everyone has a purpose, but it's up to us to discover it." I wasn't sure myself what my purpose was. All I knew was that I had a deep sincerity to see hungry people fed, homeless people sheltered, kids no longer abused, and hurting people receive relief from their pains.

The victory was bittersweet: sweet because I was on my way to engage upon a new life, but bitter because I was uncertain if I could make it in the world on my own. My past memories hadn't completely been erased. I wondered at times how different my life would be if I had one of the other kid's fathers. Old hatred kept me imprisoned, I learned. The lack of affection kept me angry. And the hunger for success (material gain) blinded me to the point that I chased after external things.

I was entering a world where every move I made had to account for something, where either success or failure was sure to show itself five years from now by view of where I sat. I was terribly afraid to face my unexpected future. No matter how bad I wanted to leave Cincinnati, the beliefs that I was now a man and ready were thoughts I had a hard time conceiving.

I Understand I Must Leave Your House

IT was my time to vacate the premises from the place I had spent my entire life, through good times and bad times. Whatever the case, history was here, and I was sure to miss it.

The echo of Dad's old deep, southern voice was heard in my head for the last time— "When you turn eighteen you gotta get outta here"—and now it was time to comply. I embraced myself mentally, careful not to exude the fear I actually possessed inside. I did my best to stand as a man in their presence, wanting to prove to each of them that I was ready to face life as a man! In an instant, flashes of what it was like never to have been a child appeared. I didn't understand why I began to think of all the things I never did with Dad or with each of them. It saddened me to remember what it was like never to have played catch with him or to simply go for a horseback ride. Then, a shout of Mom's voice caused me to break free from my hypnotic trail down memory lane.

She was extremely proud of my accomplishment. "I did it!" I told myself. The smile I always wanted to give her was upon her face! She distributed her last words of motherly wisdom as I prepared for my next-day departure to Uncle Sam's Army. In her conclusion, she continued to wrap up her sentimental goodbyes, stating, "Don't forget to *always* read Psalm 23 *The Lord is my Shepherd* from your Bible." "I won't, Mom," I assured her.

It was amazing to see how fast my life had passed before me. A child with total innocence—and in a blink of an eye, as if it were just overnight, into an adult. That is, into an adult who was unequipped and unprepared for what he was about to face.

I was thrust into the world, it seemed. In addition, I was saddened by each remembrance of every tear I cried and the neglect that had been rendered. Yet, I still hungered for my absent father. Something inside of me believed that he alone was a key ingredient to fill the void. Eagerly, I hoped to rediscover the thing possibly cancelled out by all the turmoil that took place inside my home. Something was missing from my life. Something every little child has a right to experience—their time of innocence.

"FOR EVERY MAN SHALL BEAR HIS OWN BURDENS." —GALATIANS 5:5

THIS was indeed my cross to bear. The United States Army, a Heavy Equipment Mechanic (62-B) was my occupational status. "Just my luck, a 'grease-monkey'," I said discourag- ingly to myself. I hated getting my hands dirty in the past, and now, it was mandatory for me to dirty not only my hands but my entire body. I was completely unhappy with my choice of career. Nevertheless, if it had provided a way out of Ohio, I would have enlisted as a mascot.

They called the steel cab that transported us to our base housing unit a "cattle truck." The name fit it because it truly was used for hauling cattle. We crossed the rough terrain, but not without rocking from side to side, tossing each new recruit carelessly. We all would have been better off if we had bolts in our shoes to hold us in place. Our heads were buried face down inside the heavy duffle bag to ensure that we wouldn't discover the path that led us to our destination.

The drill sergeants' shouts cut through the silent air as they did their best to exert as much intimidation as one could. I can't speak for anyone else, but it worked on me. "Don't nobody look up! Keep ya heads down inside the duffle bag, or else! You ladies belong to me now! I am your mother and your father. If you want to do anything, you ask me! Do I make myself clear?" It was certified from that moment that I had made the biggest mistake of my life.

I was upset at myself for allowing my parents to persuade me to join the Army. At times, I convinced myself it was their fault, the sole reason why I was now going through such agonizing pain. The drill sergeant's yelling never seemed to cease. From the moment we entered the compound, up until we retired for the night, the yelling continued.

I wasn't accustomed to this much authority over my life; compared to these guys, Dad was a saint. I concluded that I wasn't about to endure sixteen weeks of abuse from a bunch of big-hat, combat-boot wearing men who were on a power trip. My mind was made up, I didn't care what my family and friends thought about me, I was quitting!

The now familiar growl of the drill sergeant interrupted my moment of self-discussion, this time executing his newest command. "You ladies line up. Sit ya duffle bags on the line and get ready to receive your new haircuts."

"I'm sick and tired of everyone telling me what to do. Tired, tired, tired," I said beneath my breath. I was determined to do *as I please, when I please.* At least, that's what I was thinking in my head. Instead, I obeyed the command. I wished I could turn back the hands of time … not much, just enough to say "*NO!*" when asked if I wanted to join the Army.

The first day was a total nightmare. But no matter how bad it pained me to stay, quitting wasn't an option. I could only imagine what tomorrow would entail. Was I *truly* ready for this? It was hard for me to overlook the other men who had also gotten themselves into the same situation. I wondered if they were there of their own free will, or were they persuaded as I was? Whatever their reasons, the one thing we all had in common was that we were all about to undergo many hours of calisthenics and much physical and mental abuse from the men in charge.

It did my heart good to see the day finally end; indeed, it had been long and frustrating. And my poor body, although it was in good shape, was not ready for all of what they were attempting to execute. I was certain the night's sleep would revitalize me, certain that things would be much different in the morning, thanks to the rest I was about to receive.

The Military

"Wake up, ladies!"

THESE were the first words we heard our next morning of basic training. "This guy has to be kidding, it's 4:00 in the morning," I said to myself, yet still careful to keep moving from beneath the covers. "Get your duffle bags and meet me downstairs in thirty minutes!" he continued.

I wanted out, but it was far too late. The only way out was to either fail all of my training courses or be discharged because of bad behavior. I pondered which route I would take. Then, coming to my senses (or maybe it was letting my pride get the best of me), I decided that quitting was for wimps and losers and I was neither of those.

The first week of boot camp mainly consisted of learning how to march. I learned quickly that not everyone in this world is rhythmically coordinated. There were actually guys who appeared to have two left feet, as they say. Marching came easy for me, however. My coordination and exercise ability acquired from martial arts and playing sports as a child came in handy. But for those who were rhythmically challenged, it became their worst nightmare.

I was told by my recruiter in Cincinnati that basic training consisted of eight weeks of intensive physical measures and eight weeks of schooling. But now that I was here, face to face with these men who continued to yell, I realized that there was a lot of information my recruiter friend forgot to tell me. I vowed that when I returned to Cincinnati, I would beat the living snot out him. "The second week of this mess," I said to Erick, who had come by way of Brooklyn, New York. We both shared ill vibes pertaining to the decision we made to join the Army. The other thing we *all* shared was the soup-bowl haircuts that left us looking like multiracial space aliens, in my opinion. We marched up hills. We marched down hills. We marched around the military base. We even marched in place. I had my full share of marching, and all I could think of was getting home to Cincinnati to find that recruiter.

In addition to the constant marching, jumping jacks or side-straddle hops, as they would call them, became our number-one exercise. The regiment of exercises was something I was accustomed to but not to this extent. Nonetheless, I excelled in all they brought my way, all except following their commands. When it came to doing chores or waking up for guard duty, they could have found someone else for that. The exercise part was cool, but the wakeups in the middle of the night and constant yelling at me would cause problems our way, I knew for sure.

I wasn't well disciplined in the area of taking orders. All of my life, I rebelled against authority; partially Mom and Dad's fault for that, I wanted to blame. In any case, the drill sergeants noticed the area in which I was undisciplined. They were certain they could bring about a change, I only imagined them saying. They looked at me as if I was some sort of challenge they welcomed. There was truly a price to pay for my stubborn, rebellious, Mr. Know-It-All attitude: a price noteworthy of mention for everyone who believes that they are the toughest man alive.

Okay, I Get the Picture

IT was late that evening. We had completed every activity on our things to do list for that day's training. I had forgotten the confrontation I had with one of the officers, but he hadn't. After we had showered and prepared for bed, hoping to gain enough rest for our next day activities, out of nowhere I hear, "Private Smith, downstairs—now!"

Immediately I jumped from my rack, wearing nothing but my shorts, and rushed to see what this guy could possibly want at this time of night. "Yes, sergeant," I said, noticing the grim expression with a half smile on his face. If I could read minds, I would say that he was thinking, "Oh, how fun this is going to be!"

"Front-leaning rest positiooooon!" These were the only words he uttered that penetrated my ears as an ocean's mighty roar. I stood there puzzled before him. "What?" I responded; "Front-leaning rest position … for what?" Slow and reluctant, I made my way towards the tile floor that would be my companion for however many hours he decided. In anger, I placed both hands directly in front of me and arched my back as a cat would do who is ready to engage in battle. My buttocks lifted off the floor, aiming directly towards the sky; then, once content with my position, he began sounding off numeric cadences.

"One, two, three … one! One, two, three … two!" Each three-count was only equivalent to one set. "I'll be here all night," I said, yet careful not to break stride for fear of starting all over with the exercise. By the time he was done initiating his calisthenics program, and even some I believed he made up, I had a change of attitude. I rolled. I did leg lifts, side twists, hundreds of pushups, neck rolls, etc. You name it, I did it … and more. "Was disobedience in this case worth it?" I asked myself, especially when I realized there was no chance of winning.

The next day I moved eagerly to be among the first to arrive downstairs for formation. "I get the picture," I said to myself. I was determined never to undergo anymore of the drill sergeant's corrective tactics. "No way must I continue to learn a lesson through forced measures," I told myself. I awoke the next morning thirty minutes before anyone, ready to face the new day's challenges, some of which I was sure to dread. We were told that our fourth week of training would consist of marching fifteen miles. Always confident in my physical fitness ability, I welcomed this challenge, determining that this would surely display what I was made of.

Halfway through the basic training there were many guys who "just couldn't cut it," as they say. Many failed entirely because of the exercises regimens; then there were those who just couldn't handle the mental stress. Admittedly, I hated those sergeants. "They're always screaming," I said to myself. Even though they had punished me somewhat severely that night, my rebellious attitude still tried to hang on to some of its old nature. There was just too much residue lying at the bottom, too much deposited from the many years of negative living and, of course, dear ole Dad. Things weren't about to completely changed overnight, I knew very well. But for right now, I convinced myself, I'd best let 'em have their way. "I'm not anybody's chump," I told Erick, still trying to hold on to what little pride I had left. "Yeah, man, the night endeavor had impact, but they haven't completely broken me; I'm much tougher than that," I implied, trying to convince him that I was too tough to be broken.

It was nothing for me to help those who were unable to climb the hills or even going to the rear to march with other men who were unable to keep up with the fast pace. But I couldn't wait until boot camp was over. Yet there were still three and a half weeks of this phase remaining before the school phase. In the school phase, we were to learn about our specific job, the core to why any of us joined in the first place.

We weren't permitted to go off camp grounds until we reached our military occupational skill (MOS) phase, and that would also be an eight-week course. That I could handle, mainly because there would be a time of stress release at the Enlisted Men's Club where we could drink our heart's content. I thirsted for a nice cold beer. It had been almost two months since my last taste, and I couldn't wait!

The shower was well needed. Afterwards, I lay on my rack to catch a moment's rest from enduring an exhausting day. I stared into the air with my eyes fixed upon the discolored ceiling, as if doing so would bring me closer to home. I could clearly hear Mom's voice in my head saying, "Read Psalm 23, *the Lord is my shepherd*. When you feel like you are alone, always read that chapter." The mere thought forced me to pull a smile through the hard shell of my face, replacing the dismal expression of dread that anyone who came in my direction could notice. A sense of peace accompanied the tear in my eye. I felt the loving arms of her embrace I had been waiting a long time to receive. It didn't matter that it wasn't a physical touch; I knew that her presence was there with me. I crawled beneath the wool covers that blanketed me with a new spirit of peace I had obtained. There were no more memories of the day I just endured, and before I knew it, I drifted into a deep sleep, the first since my arrival.

The absence of telephone use until our fourth week added to the strain of surrendering to the drill sergeant's instructions. The unwanted, added pressure, I believe, impeded my ability to adapt, making my transition arrive at turtle's pace.

I needed desperately to hear Mom's voice, confident she would say the right thing to soothe the heartache inside of her number seven child who was in dire need of returning to the breast of the woman who had birthed him. She was the only person able, at the time, to reconstruct the broken and lonely spirit I harbored inside. Dad wanted me to be a man, but my only remembrance of what a man was supposed to be drank beer, hung on street corners, beat the women they said they loved, and sold drugs.

The training was far from over. However, we were now permitted to make a long-awaited phone call! I needed some revitalization, some new energy that would help me make it through the mandatory second phase in order to graduate. It was our day, and as soon as we were released to do so, I gave Mom a call. "Hello, Mom, how are you? The training? Well, these drill sergeants have pricked my last nerve."

"Are you reading your Bible?" she asked.

"Yes," I responded.

"It's almost over, baby; soon you'll be back at home. But, until then, keep your head up, do what they tell you, and know that Jesus loves you."

"I know. Love you, too, Mom," I replied as I sadly hung up the receiver.

I took her advice at face value and started reading my Bible much more than I had in the past. I started with Psalm 23 just as she had suggested, not really sure as to what I should receive from the scriptures. I tried to follow the Bible commands as best I could, especially the ones that spoke of taming the tongue and controlling the temper. Besides, those were the most important to me at the time, since my current situation mandated that I learn to do so or continue to make my four months a living nightmare.

I had seen other guys in the unit adamantly oppose the drill sergeant's commands, but not without receiving their share of perpetual brutality. Day after day these guys just refused to comply. At least I was smart enough to know when to stop bucking against a no-win situation. Sure, I too received my fair share, but enough was enough!

It was a sad event for some. Those who were insistent on rebelling paid severely. There were guys who became so disoriented from the intense training that they literally lost their minds. The end of their basic training career was spent inside of a special-unit dorm for behaviorally challenged soldiers. "I could never see that happening to me," I said, and decided to see things their way—at least for the moment.

I was rewarded for my new conduct. Since I was now able to follow orders, I was promoted to squad leader of our unit. Truthfully, it was an exciting opportunity. Not for a long time had I felt this good about achieving anything; I had to tell Mom!

THE ENLISTED MEN'S CLUB

THE beer I longed for was a thirst quencher! "Aw, just like old times," I thought, times when my crew and I would go to the neighborhood store to cop our favorite forty-ounce bottle of Old English 800, considering it "just what the doctor ordered!"

They called it the Enlisted Men's Club, although it wasn't a club solely for men; there were women present, as well—women from all over the United States who could probably drink any average man under the table. It didn't take long before I discovered how true my assumptions were. There were ladies present that could drink the average man under the table! Despite their appearance in uniform, they were quite attractive.

The second phase of training offered fewer restrictions. In this phase, we were permitted to go off base for the entire weekend. Then, as soon as we completed this phase, graduation was the ultimate achievement.

I looked forward to graduating, knowing it would bring some form of satisfaction in my life and perhaps grant me opportunity to excel beyond the lifestyle I left in Ohio: drinking, partying, sniffing cocaine ... simply just wasting time.

Tim had successfully achieved his goal in the United States Air Force, bringing pure joy to Mom's heart. I sought to provide for her that same feeling of elation in hopes to openly display that she hadn't failed as a mother. I gave my all toward the career field for which I had enlisted and kept all of my extracurricular activities where they belonged: tucked away in my own little secret closet.

The course was much more difficult than I imagined. In addition to the grease that splattered all over me, the w o r k book read as a foreign language. Bottom line: I didn't understand. That made following the instructions inside the manual all the more difficult. Then there was the cold weather. "How am I going to work on a tractor-trailer in the cold?" I asked myself. "I'm not," I said, holding firm to my final decision. I told myself that I would change my job, if possible, at the first available opportunity.

It was best that I changed occupation rather than fail. Failing meant you could be discharged for educational reasons. I couldn't stand to see that on my military file, so I applied for a job change. It was denied, for what reason. "I can pass this course," I said quietly, hoping to give myself the psychological boost of confidence I needed. However, my dilemma was, "Do I even really care to try?" ending my self-discussion.

We were provided two chances to pass if we should fail, but even that wasn't a satisfying comfort to someone who didn't like his occupation in the first place. Failing the second time would surely provide a way out; either you'd be assigned to a not-so-difficult career, or you could apply for a military discharge that couldn't hurt your career on the outside. I decided whichever route I took, it was all right with me.

Unfortunately, I must have spoken my fate into existence

because not more than three weeks into the training, I was told by the class instructor that I had not passed the written part of the test. I was given a second chance just as they had promised, and this time, I'd pass. Failing the first time meant a week held back, only to impede your graduation date. To fail a second time meant you were headed back to the dorm to pack your belongings and wait to depart back to your hometown.

Erick, from Brooklyn, New York, exhausted all of his chances. No longer could he test nor train with another class; it was over for him. We shared our goodbyes back at the dorm that night as he packed for his return to Brooklyn. I wondered if I would ever see him again. I concluded that I had made a good friend, in any case.

The setback turned out to be a good thing for me. It allowed me to gain a better understanding, due in part to the instructor's willingness to give me more assistance the second time around.

He wanted me to pass. In fact, he wanted everyone to pass, I truly believe.

I had come a long way since my arrival to Fort Leonard Wood, Missouri. That bad attitude, temper tantrum of a child finally felt like an adult. No more was I the entertainment at night for the drill sergeants. Whether I cared to believe it at the time or not, my regular Bible reading schedule gave substance to my once inward, despondent life. There was meaning and direction in my life now, I told myself— at least for the moment.

(I'm a witness that change doesn't come overnight. And no matter how hard you try, that old evil nature will fight profusely to prohibit you from becoming the man or woman you're trying to become. Don't be discouraged — keep pressing; I did!)

The training reached its final week, and soon those who had successfully completed the program could stand with their heads held high in the presence of their friends or family members. The event would undoubtedly be a memorable occasion, for me especially if Mom and Dad were on site to witness my accomplishment.

Up to this point, everything in my life had been procured by my own means. No one directed me or assisted me in the choices I should make. Thus far, all of my successes and failures came through trial and error. If I succeeded it was through trial; and if I failed, it was also from trial… trial and error.

Eagerly I rushed to the phones to call home in hopes to hear that Mom and Dad would be attending this special moment. As conversation proceeded, all I could remember hearing were the words, "Unfortunately, baby, we won't be able to attend, but congratulations." Anger and disappointment sliced bitterly. And instantly, their absenteeism proved to give way to pain and heartache once again.

I closed the door of my mental conversation. Despite their mention of failure to appear, I regained grips with my emotions and contended that it really wasn't important. Although some part of me was still disappointed, I tried to appease myself by rationalizing their absence. I reminded myself that all through my life I had not had their support, and concluded, "So why should this be any different?"

They believed I had accepted their neglect calmly. That, for whatever it was worth, no more was I the little kid that left home. With grace, I mentioned that I would see if Tim would be willing to support me. "I'm sure he could make it," I told myself. He lived near Chicago, Illinois. I really did want at least one of my family members present.

Later that evening, I called to see if he would be available, if by any chance his schedule would allow him to get away for a few days. My heart was set on this occasion, and disappointment would have indeed had its impact if none of my family members were there to share in my joy.

"Hey, Tim, watsup?" opening the conversation.

"Nothing," he said in response, "Just, you know, staying alive."

"Hey, listen," I said, "My military graduation is coming up, and Mom and Dad aren't able to make it. I was wondering—that is, if your schedule permits—would you come support me? It would really mean a lot to me."

He accepted my invitation with no hesitation. I wanted to see him. It had been a long while since we last saw each other.

Many of us decided to spend our last and final weekend off base at one of our homes away from home, a house for prostitutes. We'd collectively ante up any money and set sail for the fun houses. Yet it never failed, after the weekend splurge was over, we'd return to the base pennyless, reciting the same song time after time, "How could we give those tricks our money… *every* weekend?" knowing very well that as soon as the following weekend rolled back around, we were going right back to do the same thing again. Whom were we kidding?

Time was of the essence now. For all who had begun and completed the necessary requirements in order to be considered a certified soldier in Uncle Sam's Army, the weekend to come would give each individual some merit and good standing back in their hometown. I reminisced at how the drill sergeants had taken a group of uncoordinated, unruly, hard-headed men from different parts of the country, brought each of us together, and instituted harmony. WOW! Amazing!

I laughed at the recollection of my first day at the base, headed towards the steel cab, the "cattle-truck." I smirked at the remembrance of hearing the drill sergeant yell at the top of his lungs, "Front leaning rest positiooon," stretching the last part of the word for impact and assurance that everyone heard (that left a great imprint in my mind). Good memories were attached to the hard training, somewhat explaining to me that life isn't easy, but hard times don't always last. That was the lesson I received.

But it was the nights at the Enlisted Men's and Women's Club, drinking the ice-cold beer that had frost seeping through the beer mug that I remembered most. Even the long marches in the scorching hot sun headed for the hand-grenade site or weapons' site appeared to have been all worth it!

You could hear the roars from the excited soldiers who made it through, every cadet anxiously waiting to interact with their family, ready to move from cadet status to soldier status! We were all excited! Each man rendered an early morning salute to the other. Anxiety and anticipation were felt in the atmosphere in a manner never before felt. The spirits were high, and even the drill sergeants, whom we had before considered evil tyrants, embraced us with warmth and admiration.

I'M A SOLDIER NOW!

THE graduation banners were hung high in the air, and the crowd of people who had appeared to witness this occasion sparkled with glee. Before the initial commencement, the men had time to fellowship with their families and share some of the highlights of their experiences. "What an atmosphere," I thought, "If only Mom and Dad were here." I would have loved for them to see me in my uniform. How proud I looked standing there with surety because of my accomplishment. "But it's okay," I decided, "my big brother Tim is here, and he is as good as any."

It was at least a two-hour event. But once ended, Tim treated me to a great weekend in the city. I had developed some good relationships while in boot camp, often wishing that Erick from Brooklyn, New York was standing with me to receive his certificate of completion, as well. But I understood, *que sera sera*, meaning "What will be, will be," as they say.

Everyone that signed up for active-duty status would receive their papers to go on to their assigned duty stations throughout the country or possibly overseas. "Not me," thinking to myself, "I'm going home, back to Cincinnati, Ohio, where I have hopes of entering college at the university."

After the exciting weekend with Tim, it was time to make arrangements for my flight. I knew that when I returned home there would be an entourage of people waiting to greet me, some there with good intentions to wish me well in my endeavor, and others, of course, there to simply speak death into my life with ill feelings toward me and everything I strived to accomplish. There were literally folks who disliked me so much that, if given a chance, would have killed me. I discovered that everyone who claimed to be my running buddy and close friend was really my enemy in disguise.

For the first time in my life, it had appeared that the plan *I* had created for *my* life was falling into alignment. "Nothing could possibly go wrong," I said, emotionally energized. I was a full-fledged man now, I thought. "After undergoing the type of training that I just completed, I'm ready to take on the world!" I said, proud, absolutely proud of *my* accomplishment!

ALL MAPPED OUT

THE plan was mapped out. I would attend college at the university with my major geared towards psychology; I'd be a child psychologist. That was a hidden desire. I also figured I would remain in the Army Reserve while attending school. Then, as life continued to move forward, I would become my own boss. What a plan! I knew it wasn't going to be easy to detach myself from the old habits and peers. But I also knew that if I was going to become successful in life, those old friends I once associated with would need to be put in the rear of my life.

Nothing has changed here

THE flight was smooth and relaxing. With the exception of an air pocket that scared the heck out of me, all was well. The flight also provided time for me to gather my thoughts, to categorically arrange the well thought out plan *I* had drafted. This was my new opportunity, I believed. A chance to take full advantage of a plethora of opportunities that awaited me. I was the proud, upright soldier returning home for the first time in months. "I'll show them," I said, displaying a partial smile on my face as if satisfaction had been achieved. Ending my in-depth conversation with myself, I returned my focus again to the plane ride. Over the airplane's intercom came the announcement I waited anxiously to hear. "We are now approaching Greater Cincinnati Airport; please fasten your seat-belts."

"I'm finally home, and this time, to stay!" I said, relieved to be out of the air.

I understood that I hadn't been gone very long, but a lot

inside me had changed. I wondered if the fellas I left behind had changed as well. But what did I really expect? Coming to grips with my own questioning, I realized that the life we all lived was our reality. "So why would they change?" I ended, allowing truth to outweigh wishful thinking. The ride home to my parents' house took forever, it seemed. Perhaps longer than the plane ride, I thought. Nonetheless, I was finally home! **Ready, ready, ready!** for whatever life wanted to toss my way. "I'm a man now, an Army soldier; I can handle anything!"

I was anxious to exit the yellow taxicab and the driver who took his time getting me to my destination. Once in front of my parents' house, I quickly recognized the same faces standing in the same area as when I left for the military. James was the very first person my eyes fixed on. Those to whom I was close upon leaving to play in Uncle

Sam's Army were excited to see me. They greeted me with the usual accommodations we always indulged in. There were forty ounces of our favorite drinks already cracked open. I wanted one desperately, but I knew that Mom would kill me if I went off somewhere with the fellas to get high before sitting down with her to engage in a conversation. She had missed her baby, she told me, her number seven child. Knowing she'd be hurt if I left, I put the invitation on hold for a while.

My first month home from active-duty status went fairly well.

I had endured, thus far, all of the challenges I faced and held to the newly received principles induced by Uncle Sam. The transition at this point was going in the right direction, I thought, but access into the university came at a much slower pace.

Things didn't appear to be moving along as quickly as I had predicted. My well thought out plan wasn't coming together the way I expected it to take shape. However, entrance into the Army Reserve was overnight, it seemed. They phoned to give me a schedule regarding the hour I was required to report for duty, just hours after my return home, as if they had a wire attached to me informing them of my arrival. As for schooling, which was my primary goal, it seemed as if there was an evil blockade prohibiting me from enrolling. The job search was also proving to be a failed attempt. For whatever reason, I kept ending up with the short end of the stick. Why I didn't return to the life insurance company is beyond me. I guess it was due to my impaired thinking ability.

I had been home one month already and still there was no clear sign that *my* plan was about to be manifested. To say I was frustrated would be an understatement. I was fed up with the weekend trips to Fort Thomas, Kentucky to work on some equipment the actual name of which I still hadn't learned. My job searches were tiresome and unproductive. Having more failures than successes, I suddenly came to the realization that I may as well do nothing for a while. "Take a break," I thought to myself. Why not? I earned it. Besides, I really didn't like the career field anyhow. I was looking for more reasons to justify my defiant actions of never returning to Fort Thomas. I agonized over how I might terminate my career.

It was a few months before Mom noticed that my old friends and familiar environment were having a dynamic effect on me, resurrecting that old behavior. It wasn't difficult for her, I guess, to notice the drastic change that was occurring. Adamantly, she insisted I take a self-analysis of my life or else I would have to leave their home. She continued to say that "Madisonville, and all of your old running buddies are interfering with your decision-making and impeding your possible, future success ... cut 'em loose!" I really didn't care to hear what she had to say again. Nonetheless, this time I put up no defense on their behalf. I recalled her saying those exact words in the past when she swore that I should only hang with Geggy.

A moment of clarity entered, I suppose, because I found myself agreeing with everything she had said. Coming to grips with myself, I realized that I was drinking excessively again and my same old behavior was projecting itself. "I am headed for destruction," I said, to myself, confirming Mom's statement. "Mom is correct," I thought, and knew that if I didn't leave Madisonville, I'd end up in a lot of trouble.

Many hindrances were there to ensure that I never achieve anything constructive—that I would undoubtedly stand a great risk of becoming just like the individuals I swore to *never* imitate. Mom insisted I take an alternative route, reminding me that I had come too far to allow other people to mess it up. Her words didn't fall on deaf ears, I assured her, and promised that I would go see the Army Recruiter first thing in the morning to see if active duty was possible. After receiving the information needed in order to enlist on full-time status, I was unable to restrain the anticipation. Just as before, I rushed to share the news with Mom, knowing that she would also be overjoyed!

I never let go of my promise to her: to attend church. Sunday served as my day of repentance. And since all I had to do was attend, I should've been in great standings with the Big Guy, I supposed.

Dad remained indifferent, as always, not saying much as to which direction I should take. At one point, I really didn't think he even cared … as long as I was leaving *his* home. he had simmered down, not as fierce as in the past. But the fatherly advice I still looked to receive resided in his own personal, locked-away vault that no one was permitted to enter. Yet there was a feeling I had inside that told me he was proud. And even if he wouldn't acknowledge it openly, I believed it and that was enough for me. I realized I couldn't expect a miracle. And as I had learned by-way of the military, "change don't come overnight." For the first time in my life, I could honestly say that I was proud of his efforts!

THE SECOND TIME AROUND

BEING prior military definitely proved to be just what I needed! It granted access to roam the entire campground! And the fact that I didn't have to endure another basic training gave new meaning to the word "elated." I felt for the cadets who were just starting the training, remembering when not too long ago I was in their same shoes. I chuckled and quivered at that thought.

The fact that I was prior military also required that I take on a new military occupational skill (MOS). The next two months at Fort Leonard Wood, Missouri, for the second time around, would be exciting and experimental, I knew for sure. I took full advantage of the new liberty. Daily I headed to the other side where the female cadets lived in hopes to "strike gold," as we called it. Eureka! I thought, while approaching a sexy female. I introduced myself, sure to mention that I was "prior military," certain that would give me more leverage in obtaining my goal to engage in an off campus rendezvous.

I expressed my interest in learning her name and further implied that, "It would be a good idea if we met off base to participate in a little off-post entertainment." Almost immediately she accepted my proposal. "Yes!" I said in my mind, hoping my thoughts hadn't escaped me. That would have allowed her to notice my enthusiasm. I didn't want her to think she had me, you know.

She was from Baltimore, Maryland. "Maryland," I said, "What's in Maryland?" Not realizing I was demonstrating my ignorance pertaining to history, she pleasantly explained and did so with patience, I might add, before I realized that Maryland was, for the most part, next to New York . I also learned that it was a highly historical state, and so on and so on.Feeling quite embarrassed I wondered, "Where was I during that part of history class?"

It was apparent we were enjoying each-other's company during our weekend stays in the city, growing closer on each occasion and sharing intimate details regarding the reasons why we joined the military. As conversations emerged deeper, I learned that she had two young kids, a boy and a girl, the girl being older. I also found out that just as I had planned, she too had only joined the Army Reserves. After her training was over, she'd head back to Baltimore, Maryland, where her plans were to continue providing for her young kids. I found that admirable.

I knew in my spirit, we'd be separating after that conversation, mainly because I was now active duty and there was no telling where they'd send me. Furthermore, I knew that I had no intentions on maintaining a long-distance relationship with anyone. Therefore, I thought it would be best if we put a little distance between us to ensure that no one gets hurt. That sounded like a good plan and we both made every effort to stick to the original agreement. But as a week or two passed by, we found our way back in each other's presence, headed for the city again. There were only two weeks left for me at Fort Leonard Wood until my departure elsewhere, possibly even overseas. I was sure this was the end of our relationship. We promised to enjoy the final weeks we had left with each other. Each week we headed to the hotel. Once there, I'd make up some bogus excuse as to why I needed to leave. My objective was to see if I could find some powder cocaine, but surely, I couldn't reveal that part of my life to her. Like any dope fiend would do, I lied. It had been a while since my last toot, I told myself, justifying my actions to gratify my addiction. I didn't know I was addicted but found out later that just because I didn't indulge daily didn't mean I wasn't addicted.

Upon my return to the hotel room, she questioned my whereabouts. I commended her for not being persistent, for letting the answer I gave her be just that. Then, in a second thought, I determined that it really didn't matter much to me anyhow if she had discovered my dark secret; the simple fact was that within a week we'd never see each other again anyway. My assigned duty station notice arrived during my last week of schooling. I was going to miss her, I knew. And I was unable to convince myself of anything different. I knew that if I could see her again, I would. I completed this career field with ease. A transportation operator, this time (64 Charlie, they called it). I hadn't minded learning to drive the eighteen-wheelers and Hummers, a.k.a. Humvees. I felt comfortable driving the vehicles, especially the Hummers. I was amazed at how they went through the mud and deep waters with such ease. That alone inspired me to continue the occupational career granted me this time around. The only drawback to being prior military was that I was not permitted to participate in the festive graduation ceremony this time. That was a disappointment. You could only graduate once from boot camp. I guess I wanted everyone to know that I had done something meaningful. Even if they didn't know me personally, they could see my current accomplishment.

I made a point to be present at her graduation, wishing her well and mentioning that I hoped she'd have a prosperous life, careful not to forget to mention her young kids. When the night of events came to its end, I and a few other GIs made tracks back to the dorm. There I would discover a paper on my rack. At first glance, I perceived it to be a letter from home. I grabbed the sheet of paper, not fully comprehending the contents it contained, yet noticed the writing and heading that read, *Military Deployment*. Slowly, I moved my eyes across the page, thinking that the slower I read the document, the more it would make sense. Then I noticed, located near the bottom of the page, the words informing me as to my assigned duty station. "Fort Meade, Maryland!" I said, loudly in shock. "I can't believe it!" I had actually been assigned to a military intelligence brigade. "Maryland, it must be fate!" I said, anxious to tell her the good news.

The next day I raced to tell her where I had been assigned.

The news was received actually much better than I imagined. She implied how excited she was that our relationship would continue. She stated how she'd take me on a tour and show me what Maryland was really about. "I'm truly looking forward to exploring Baltimore," I told her; "but my first priority is to settle in at my new camp."

"I understand," she kindly replied. "But call me as soon as you arrive in Maryland … can you at least give me that much?"

"Of course," I said, smiling, and assured her of my word. "See you in Maryland," I said, giving her a kiss on the cheek and politely turning away to go prepare for my departure in the morning.

ACCESS TO THE PENTAGON ... ME!

FORT Meade was an intelligence post, a base that housed counterespionage agents. It was required that everyone assigned to that unit receive a clearance, either secret or top secret. No one could enter the intelligence building without proper identification.

I reported for duty the following morning as instructed. The motor pool was my assigned post. My instructions were to report to the sergeant in charge, a Panamanian who looked as if he was completely African-American. As he went through his routine for all new recruits, I scanned the area and noticed that there weren't any cars on the lot that would blow an agent's cover. All of the vehicles were completely civilianized.

Weeks into my new career, my potential to be efficient, well kept, and groomed in my military uniform was observed. I was chosen out of several other men to exclusively provide transportation for the brigade colonel, the command sergeant-major, and other high-ranking officials. Not only did I consider my position an honor, but also a reward for my turn-around attitude.

The new position required me to obtain a security clearance level of secret status. This clearance gave me access to many areas prohibited to individuals without. It was noted that I would have to make trips to Washington, DC's Pentagon. The information needing to be transported was highly confidential. This job was extremely exciting! I couldn't believe that I was actually walking around our nation's Pentagon! I handled many highly classified documents and also worked in a secondary position of requisitions. Life had new meaning!

I spent much of my time all over the east coast. Delaware was a beautiful state. Maryland and DC became my homes away from home.

Brooklyn, New York served as my weekend fix! And let's not forget Baltimore, or "B'more," as they call it; there was still much unfinished business that needed to be handled there: my female friend, Jennifer.

I was learning the different cities like the back of my hand from all of the extensive driving. Each successful trip gave me new status with the colonel. He alone had a one-on-one opportunity to witness my dedication and commitment which quickly earned me my first promotion. I was now promoted to the rank of Private First Class or PFC in military lingo. What a momentous honor.

Celebration was long overdue; it was definitely time to give my friend a call to discuss some plans for the night. This would be our very first date since my arrival; I knew this night would have to be memorable. She was excited to hear my voice, she said. After a lengthy phone conversation, we arranged a day and time to meet. In the gap of reuniting, I found a few friends in the dorm who partied in the same manner as I. Once we discovered each other's little secret, it became customary at least twice out of the week to engage in a toot.

I arrived at her door after following the exact directions she gave me. Her excitement was heard by even the neighbors next door. After we sat awhile, we reminisced about basic training and how I ended up in Baltimore. She moseyed into the other room and closed the partition separating the bedroom from the living room, then began to get dressed for our night outing. Her attire was fitting. It wasn't anything sexy or over-dressed, but she made the jeans and blouse look exceptionally good. I, being the lust-driven maniac that I was, had all types of impure thoughts dancing harmonically through my mind.

We hit some pretty amazing party spots. However, my favorite of all was the Baltimore Harbor. The view it produced was enchanting. When the night came to its end, the only thing I could think of was how nice it would be if I had a line of cocaine. I was sure the night would be more of a success if I could just motivate myself, and the cocaine would do just that. I was determined to get the high I wanted. Even if she didn't engage, I was about to find the candy I longed for, becoming more and more adamant about feeding the desire inside. Promptly we returned to the house. I wondered if she noticed my sudden shift in spirit and possibly attitude, as well. I knew within that the urge to get high was increasing. My stay at her house wasn't long, mainly in part to my curfew at the barracks, but mostly (I strongly believe as I look at it today) due to my hunger to get high.

Extra privileges were granted because of my position as the brigade colonel's driver, and I took full advantage of all of them. I utilized the new model car with telephone attachment inside daily. It was my vehicle, and no one could tell me differently. My prideful spirit prompted me to display the telephone to my ear whenever I went through Southeast DC. I wanted everyone to see, just like most people who are trying to put up a front. Of course, the colonel wasn't in the car. He had either gotten dropped off at the Pentagon or some other classified facility. It was my time to shine for the moment, I said, and for the moment, I shined.

Many times, I transported secret, top secret, and highly classified documents to their destination without the colonel or any other high-ranking official accompanying me. The Pentagon and Arlington Hall Station were my two favorite places. Whenever I received the command to transport the documents to any particular location, my energy level always increased. The thought of knowing that I would be amongst those walking the halls of some of our country's most historical settings was unimaginable.

The trips to Delaware held their highlighted moments, as well. The restaurant we'd dine in, possessing a window seat that provided a clear view of the ocean, served as an inspiration. In all, I suppose, the fact that I had gained this level of achievement was an indescribable measure to me at the time. I felt worthy, validated;,accepted, something I had never before received. I was alive, it seemed, and felt as if God, of whom Mom always spoke, had finally answered my silent cries. "What could possibly go wrong?" I asked myself.

My female friend and I had slowed down our weekly gatherings. The direction *my* personal life was beginning to take would create problems.

The once controllable use of cocaine had grown into an every-time-we-gathered occasion, and she noticed. I still didn't think there was anything wrong with an occasional toot and a few drinks, but she saw differently.

My usage hadn't hindered my ability to function, as of yet, and more importantly, I believed hadn't put my military career in any jeopardy. Therefore, I determined, she was the one with the problem. And "If she can't handle me having a little fun, well, maybe we're better off apart," I concluded.

The barracks were a lively environment at all times. This was no different to being out in the streets. You could go to any room and find any kind of liquor you desired, not to mention other stuff. We partied day and night, awakening with a splitting headache that always accompanied the hangover.

The pace was escalating, and my once clear observation of where I stood had even begun to bring concerns my way. I did take a moment to look carefully in the mirror one time, implying that I'd make some adjustments in my daily life by attending a church in the city of Baltimore, hoping that Jennifer would be up for it. "Read Psalm 23, *the Lord is my shepherd*," those words were never forgotten.

The joyous feelings I once embraced pertaining to the military were now diminishing. I no longer held the enthusiasm to drive, or even to see the sights. Occasionally, I surrendered to the depressive state from thoughts of wondering if I would do this for the rest of my life. I also wondered if the Bible would indeed serve as my motivator, my inspiration of hope, as it had before. I read it as a form of medicine, looking to get the "quick-fix" I'd always receive.

Caught between the stages of life, trying to reach some conclusive discovery as to where my life was headed, my old, inward battle resurfaced. Just as past times had proven themselves, so likewise now would I insipidly find myself in the same spiritual whirlwind, wishing that Mom and Dad would have better equipped me before sending me out into this world where every decision I make comes with dire consequences. The barracks life was the link that kept everything alive. Every weekend, someone threw a gathering in their room. I was in desperate need for some new excitement and, as luck would have it, there were a few guys going out to the Noncommissioned Officers' Club; "just the medicine I needed." I said.

"Hold up fellas; I'm rollin' witchu. I need a night out or else I'm going to implode." I made sure to put on some first-class gear; that, I learned from the OGs. In order to catch the right fish, you need the right bait. I knew without a doubt that tonight, a fish would be caught. The other fellas were dressed to impress as well; each of us had the same purpose in mind. It was customary to place a wager on who'd "strike oil" that night. I don't want to brag, but ….

As we entered the dark setting, I was blinded by the flickering strobe lights hanging high overhead. Each of us paused to discuss our game plan, believing this would be the night. When my eyes finally adjusted to the room, I surveyed the territory I chose to go occupy. While in the midst of my search, I came in eye contact with this fine, Puerto Rican chic. Instantly, we locked in on each other.

It would have been against creed for me not to go to her table and extend a proposal to dance. The fellas would have clowned me for sure, I thought, if they saw she was digging me (a slang term for interested) and I didn't make my move in her direction. My stride was automatic, as if I sailed on a cloud to reach her. I noticed she never took her eyes off me while I was in motion. The interest was shared between us, I could easily tell. And in the back of my mind, I rejoiced from knowing that I was the first one to "strike oil!" Blinded by her beauty, I really didn't give much thought to anything else. I was certain that my lust ruled me. And not understanding that beauty could have been nothing more than an outward misrepresentation of the person beneath the shell, I allowed myself to blindly embrace her exterior. Upon arriving to her table, I immediately extended a proposal to dance. She rolled her eyes as if to say no. Nevertheless, I knew I hadn't misread her true intention. I was skilled at recognizing a woman's nonverbal communication; the OGs had taught me. As I proceeded to ask again, this time, before I could complete the sentence, "If only you buy me a drink," she said. "Of course," I responded, making sure all of my pearly whites were displayed. Truthfully, I wasn't sure what I was doing when I extended the invitation to dance. The only thing I knew for sure was that before I had left the barracks, I was lonely, and now within minutes my emptiness had been filled. Instantly, *I* determined that she was the one. Or should I say, lust" determined.

Before the night ended, we exchanged names and phone numbers. Her name was Mina. I learned that she also had a brother stationed at Fort Meade, which was the reason for her being there. Perceivably having great conversations over the telephone, we realized it was time to meet in person again. I invited her to my living quarters, all the while harboring in the back of my mind ill-gotten desires. The invitation to come was accepted with no argument. Knowing that my guest would be there in no time, I hurried to tidy up a bit. I had already considered that it was time for me to settle down. I was tired of playing the field, as they say. I wanted someone with whom to share my life. "What am I saying?" I snapped out of that crazy emotional bubble I was in. True, I was lonely, "But I just met her," I said aloud to myself.

She arrived in no time flat, looking as beautiful as she had the first night I met her. I was unable to take my eyes off her, sure that this was going to be another night to remember. If not, somehow her phone number would mysteriously get lost. We engaged in a long series of communication. And throughout our in-depth exchange of questions and answers, I discovered she had a total of three kids, ages eleven, nine and four years of age. Furthermore, I discovered that she had been involved in gang participation, such as I. The only difference was that the gang she belonged to was deadly: Latin Kings. However, it didn't end there. The topic of drugs came up. Equally sharing bits and pieces about each other's history, I realized that my drug usage appeared minimal or nonexistent. I was blown away by her integrity, and said to myself, "Anyone can change. Besides, she hasn't used in a year, from what she told me." And after examining my own screwed-up life, I asked myself, "Who am I to judge?" appeasing myself in order to come to terms with the information I just heard.

I liked her a lot in just a short time span. I figured that if she could be as forthcoming with me in the future as she had in the beginning of our relationship, she could be the one! My desire was also to meet the kids she spoke so highly of: Chastity, Sianna, and Pete were their names. Sianna and Pete were full-blooded Puerto Ricans; Chastity was Puerto Rican and Black. I gazed at their photos, imagining them with us as one, big, happy family.

Our dating phase progressively moved forward. In fact, at the start of our second week, we had already discussed moving in together. Had I known that her youngest daughter Chastity was here in Maryland already, I would have sought to meet her after our first date.

The news was shared by Mina that she and her brother were having major disagreements. By the end of the week, she needed to find some other place to live or else return to Hartford, Connecticut. After hearing what she had to say, I felt I had to do something in order to keep her from leaving Maryland. Before I knew it, and unable to stop the words coming out of mouth, "Will you marry me?" came forth.

She appeared just as stunned. I knew I liked her, but "am I in love with her enough to marry her?" I asked myself. "What in God's name have I done?" as if I was having a discussion with another person. We reached an agreement, not because we deeply loved each other, I'm sure, but out of lust, loneliness, and security purposes on her part. We tried to assure each other of our future happiness, that "things will be just fine." And within two weeks of knowing each other, we were married.

We decided it was time for the other two kids, Sianna and Pete, to join us in Maryland. Even though I had seen photos of them, I couldn't wait to see them in person. Rather than have them catch a train to the Maryland, we thought it would be best if we drove to Hartford to pick them up. Moreover, I thought that it would also give me a chance to meet her family. Her mother spoke very little English at all. And her brothers, well, were either part of the Latin Kings or just flat-out "wilin out," as they say in the streets.

Hartford was unlike anything I had seen in Cincinnati. It was kind of small in diameter, but it was fast paced at all times like New York, especially during the night hours when things really heated up in the city. The gangs became more prevalent in the night life. Specifically, the neighborhood was divided into territories, each claiming hold of the block that separated the Jamaicans from the Puerto Ricans and others.

It didn't take long for me to adapt to the environment; and before I knew it, I was going to the Spanish grocery store without an escort. The multicultural atmosphere impressed me. Unlike Cincinnati, there were mixtures of ethnic groups living in the small community. It didn't matter that the neighborhood fared small regarding land mass; the crowd of people used every opportunity to make it work in their favor. The place was flooded with Puerto Ricans; the sidewalks were unable to accommodate the volume of people wishing to use them.

This was my first real experience interacting this closely with the lifestyle I had only heard about. Even during our weekend trips to New York, I did not mingle as I had come to do with Mina's family. With the exception of her older brother Lonnie, the one in the military, everyone else appeared to be thuggish. But they were all cool people when you got to know them. For me, blending in was the easy part. I had no problem.

The several days we stayed in Connecticut were informative. I was able to learn a little more about the stranger I had recently married. It appeared from the warm welcome that everyone was happy for us. And even the kids' biological dads, whom I met, conveyed their blessings upon us. Were they happy for us, or had they been rid of a virus that found herself a sucker?

The colonel and command sergeant-major were thrilled to learn of my recent marriage. Surprisingly, one morning they called me into their office. They both acknowledged that they were aware of my marriage and inquired if I needed housing. Going further in their inquiries, the colonel asked how many bedrooms I would need to accommodate my ready-made family, "Four bedrooms, sir," I answered. Then, before I could make my way out of their office, the colonel handed me a wedding gift. I was emotionally touched by their concern and care for me. I was an outstanding soldier, always on time and meeting my destinations. I had earned a personal place in the hearts of the colonel and command sergeant-major, I knew.

It wasn't long before we were able to move into our new home. There were three bedroom, two full baths, living room, dining room, a den, and of course the kitchen in the spacious home. The kids loved it. And from the look on my wife's face, so did she. She stated that she never had a place as big as our home before, and that she would turn it into a palace. We both agreed the place could use some carpet. The next day she called the company to make arrangements to have the floors covered with her choice of carpeting, a deep Royal- Blue, a color that did create essence in the bare castle.

Things were spectacular, and all I could hope for, I thought, was right before my eyes. Life as I always envisioned it. What could possibly go wrong?

Mom and Dad were proud of my accomplishment thus far

— yeah, even Dad. Believe it or not, he and I had begun to communicate much better. I figured he no longer saw me as a loser. The news that I was now married came as a surprise to both of them. Mom exhibited much more surprise than Dad, however. The shock of it all left her speechless. Despite her surprise, she congratulated me and asked, "When can I meet her … this woman … my new daughter-in-law?"

"I'll be home this weekend, and you'll meet her then." I said. She couldn't believe that I had gone away and got married. But what really bugged her, I believe, was the fact that I didn't invite them. It was sudden for all of us, including Mina's brother, who had made mention of his discomfort with the whole thing. Yet, he stated that as long as his sister was happy then he was okay with it.

Life together as a couple and with the kids served to bemeaningful. The kids enjoyed their new home on the base and were completely comfortable with their new friends. The daily activity of drinking on both our parts was done in what it appeared to be, professional moderation, and, we both accepted that she could toot a line of cocaine with me. Sniffing cocaine wouldn't cause any damage, I thought. Yet, I had learned that there were pieces of her history missing. Like the Army recruiter in Cincinnati, she too had failed to provide me with important details about her past. She shared a lot of valuable information during our conversation, but there was something she omitted. I was about to find out what it was.

Unknowingly, I opened up the floodgates to disaster. Daily, after I would return home from work, I'd begin to find her already intoxicated, sometimes to the point of excess. We both loved to drink, and together we'd often engage. But as time continued, bringing our first year of marriage to a close, drinking increased on both our parts. I thought about the information she had shared with me in the beginning of our relationship, how she once was addicted to drugs. Not putting any focus on the drinking aspect of addiction, I considered it to be okay. Before I knew it, months had gone by and we were in our second year of marriage; all hell was beginning to break loose.

Life in the military was rewarding me all of its benefits and promises of a good life before things abruptly took a drastic turn for the worse. I had played around with the drugs far too long. Now it was their payback.

HERE COMES TROUBLE

ONE day, while my wife and I were engaging in our normal, daily routine of drinking, out of nowhere she mentioned that she wanted some cocaine. I thought to myself, this was no big surprise; we periodically shared a line or two, anyhow. Agreeing with her suggestion, I gathered the car keys and instructed her to meet me in the car. Within the same breath, I commanded Sianna to keep an eye on Pete and Chastity.

We were aware of the spots that had what we were looking for. All of the Jamaicans gathered in the hottest, drug-infested area near our military base. The fact that the location was only a half a mile down the road from our home was a true accommodation, we believed. Therefore, we held no qualms in making the trip.

Once we arrived at the spot in which we were to "cop our candy," I motioned with my hand for her to get out and make the purchase. It was my fear that I might be seen by someone in the military. She did as I asked, and within seconds, it seemed, was back inside of the car. I wasn't aware she had considered another method for us to get high. When we arrived at the house, in no time was I informed of her alternative to powder cocaine.

I was ready for my energy booster; my mouth was salivating, and my nerves were recklessly out of control. I reached for the item I noticed she had cupped in her hand. She quickly withdrew to resist my advance. Administering a partial smile and speaking with her Puerto Rican accent, she said, "Papi, I have something different."

"What is it?" I asked, in a mild frustration because I felt she was hindering me from getting high.

"Well, it's cocaine, but it's in a rock form," she replied.

"Rock form, what is a rock form?" I asked, this time a little more irritated by her delay.

She opened the hand that concealed the rock of cocaine. "Have you ever done this before?" she asked.

"I have never even seen cocaine in that form," I responded. She then proceeded to provide me with a crack history lesson, as if she had majored in chemistry. Then, breaking me off a small piece that came accompanied with a seductive smile, she strolled in the direction of the trash can. Lifting the lid to the trash container, I noticed her retrieving an empty beer can from inside.

"What is that empty beer can for?" I asked.

"Just watch," she said, with that same seductive smile on her face.

I realized that there was no way for me to sniff the rock she had given me; therefore, I searched for any object that would allow me to crush my share. It didn't work. There were still particles too large for me to sniff through my nostrils.

She hadn't wasted any time. She prepped the beer can she

had retrieved from the trash. First, she punctured holes in the top and along the sides; next, she scattered cigarette ashes on the top. She made sure that her cigarette lighter was nearby in position for when that part of the preparation stage was ready to begin. She also made every effort to convince me that I was missing out on a great thing. She found humor in the fact that I wasn't utilizing the crack in its correct manner.

"Would you like some help?" she asked.

"No thanks," I answered. That was the answer she needed to hear, I guess, because no sooner had I submitted my rejection when automatically I noticed the lighter that once sat on the countertop was now in her hand, headed towards the can. *Swoosh*. I could hear the sound as the flame made connection with the crack. The lighter, it appeared, was turned up to maximum level. I starred in amazement, wondering, "What the heck is she doing?" (Except my vocabulary was completely different in those days).

As I watched her inhale the smoke from the can, she mechanically released her finger on the opposite side for better effect, she mentioned afterwards.

"You're crazy," I said, in bewilderment. "I'll stick to my sniffing."

She laughed at me as I continued my experiment, knowing that I wasn't going to receive any high from sniffing the rocks. "What's so funny?" I asked, wondering what she had found so hilarious.

Again, she skillfully placed some smaller pieces of crack on the beer can, only this time she extended the invitation my way, which I knew she would, eventually. "No thanks, I'll stick to sniffing," I said, again, repeating what I had told her before. Again, she didn't seem to care. "More for me," I only imagined her saying to herself. Once again, she found her forbidden pleasure. And, I suppose, I had opened Pandora's Box.

I noticed she began to move energetically around the house, very agitated, and as if she were unable to settle down. I didn't like what I was observing. "Powder cocaine had never made me act like that. What was in that stuff?" I thought.

The night offered little sleep for us both, but mainly for my wife. She was "wired for sound," as they say. I was determined never to touch what she had gotten a hold of, especially after witnessing the effects. "For tonight, I'd be better off drinking my liquor and going straight to sleep," were my words of comfort to myself.

The new morning was almost unmemorable, as if no drug activity took place in the home just the night before. My wife pursued the new day with normality. Getting Sianna and Pete ready for school was one of her first morning priorities. There wasn't much mention as to the activity of yesterday. Besides my stomachache and a slight head-ache, things were normal. Truthfully speaking, all except for the crack cocaine, which at least for me was new, the day was the same.

I called in to my command post officer, Sergeant Jones, and told him that I wouldn't be able to make it to work, and could he ask another driver to fill in for me? The hangovers were bad. But I didn't tell him that I had a hangover, I just said that I didn't feel well.

I noticed my nightlife activity climbing steadily. The fact that I was into my second year of a new marriage, with kids, whose entire welfare depended solely on my complete ability to function, added pressure. It was routine for me to stop at the nearest convenient store to pick up my usual twelve-pack of Budweiser beer after completing my military obligations with the colonel. Things were beginning to side-track. My drinking had become so normal that I found myself drinking even in the mornings before work.

I was losing focus; and some of the guys I used to hang with in the barracks also noticed my shifting. My personality had changed, some of them mentioned. I knew I was drinking more, but never did I notice a personality change. In my own mind, things weren't actually as bad as they implied.

I had finally completed another week of dragging myself to work, feeling the energy sapped out of me. I was drained, not only in my physical body but also spiritually. I pulled into the driveway of our home and, as always, Sianna and Pete were there to greet me. They were a delight to come home to, and my precious baby girl, Chastity, I'm sure, was somewhere, not far away.

It wasn't long before my wife recognized that I was home from work, and as always, greeted me with a kiss. Whenever she wasn't too inebriated, she'd always ask if there was anything she could do for me. She wanted me to feel relaxed after a full day's work. Noticing the paper sack that contained the twelve-pack of beer, she grabbed it and headed straight for the refrigerator, stating, "When it's time for our first throat quencher, they will be nice and cold!"

Within an hour, we were engaged in our session of entertaining our house guests. But first, she always made sure the kids had what they needed, so that there wouldn't be any interruption. I couldn't even begin to party until my favorite tunes of Frankie, Beverly, and Maze were in the stereo. That was my peace mechanism. The melody soothed my inner man, removing any problems I may have incurred throughout my workday. Frankie was my musical medicine.

The idea to go and "cop" was once again suggested by my wife as soon as the guests departed. I wanted some powder myself; therefore, I thought to myself, "That idea doesn't sound too bad!" Before agreeing to her suggestion, we made sure the kids were properly in their places, informing them of our return in a few minutes. Sianna, being the oldest, as always held the responsibility of babysitting.

Immediately entering the slew of project complexes (by this time, all of the drug dealers were familiar with our car), we were noticed by the gentleman we had dealt with on other occasions. I hadn't introduced myself as of yet to anyone. My wife carried the sole responsibility of making all transactions. Heck, truthfully, I had more confidence in her ability than I had in my own. Her background undoubtedly certified her.

We left the unlit area quickly, not out of fear but because both of us wanted to hurry home to commit ourselves to each one's drug of choice. This left little time for straggling in the neighborhood. As soon as we pulled into the driveway, she exited the car much faster than I had, not even allowing the vehicle to come to a complete stop. I wasn't far behind, right on her heels. I was determined not to let her enter the house before me, partially believing she would cheat me out of my share of the purchase. She had bought cocaine in rock form the last time, and this time, I was determined to have my powder.

She headed, once again, directly to the trash can in order to retrieve an empty beer can. I was familiar with her ritual by now. In rare form, she administered the same ritual as always. First, the can; second, the holes punctured in the top and the sides; third, the ashes recovered from finished cigarettes; then, finally, her crack on top of the ashes. Now she was ready!

"You bought crack again," I said to her in fury. "I told you I wanted powder!" I was growing angrier and angrier at each thought of her neglect of my wishes. *I could kill you*, I thought. "Just give it to me," I said in fury.

This was hard, but I really wanted to get high this time. I learned from the last time that getting a high from sniffing the rock cocaine wasn't going to happen. Glancing at my wife proceeding to flicker the cigarette lighter onto the piece of cocaine, thoughts of trying it her way danced in my head. Suddenly, as if she heard my thoughts, she asked if I wanted to try some. I remembered her offer the last time and my firm stance toward her. However, before answering this time, I hesitated. I was somewhat curious as to what the cocaine would do if I consumed it her way, but more so "feaning" from the desire to get high.

She choked after taking a long inhale from the can. I had to laugh. The look on her face gave way to pallor. Her eyes widened immediately, as if to say she had just been surprised or as a deer caught in headlights. I hadn't noticed that reaction before; now I was really curious.

WHY DID I GIVE IN?

"All right," I said, "Let me try it." I gave in.

She smiled, as if I was a genie who had just granted her favorite wish. "Let me hold it, Papi." she said, carefully placing each finger in its appropriate location to ensure that no air could enter the can while I was in the midst of my first lesson of smoking crack cocaine. "Hold it in!" she exclaimed, with enthusiasm to be giving me my lesson.

I could feel the smoke rushing to my brain. Then, after a brief ten-second hold of the smoke in my lungs, I exhaled. The dizziness took over me and all I could do was stand still. This time, the joke was on me. She laughed ecstatically. The feeling was unusual. I liked it within the first thirty seconds of exhaling, but shortly after, an uncontrollable urge took over me. I was unable to relax. That feeling I didn't like.

The new way of consuming cocaine had its pros and cons, I mentioned. Nevertheless, the *pros* caused me to engage deeper and deeper, day after day. The day-to-day activities served merely as something to do during our leisure time, I thought. What a trap, I found that to be.

Weeks and months had vanished quickly, and my responsibility and my behavior streamlined in the direction of negligence. The more we engaged in our newfound high, the more it intensified, even if I was unaware of it doing so. My inability to perform my military duties was noticed throughout my unit. Questions were raised as to if I was smoking crack cocaine; opposingly, I denied. My roommate, a kid from Miami, Florida, mentioned to me that they suspected me of using drugs. It appeared I ignored him, but in the back of my mind, I knew I was getting in way over my head.

I didn't realize that I was becoming hooked on the drug. All I could see was that the new enjoyment had escalated to a daily way of life for my wife and me. The kids even recognized that they were being neglected. That was never my intent to neglect the little ones. But what do you do when your number one priority in life is to get high?

Things progressively shifted for the worse. My marriage began to rapidly fall apart. Instead of enjoying each other's company, as we had done in the beginning of our relationship, now we were fighting on a regular basis. The kids watched at times, and at times even found themselves in the center of our mess. Sianna was my little peacekeeper, often telling her mom to stop provoking me.

My military career was taking flight towards destruction, as well. I had lost all control, it seemed. I wanted to make it to my exercise training, but the chemical reaction I got from the crack cocaine wouldn't release me. My attendance for physical training (PT) had reached a state of barely or nonexistent. Everyone was aware of the severity of my addiction, by now (and it didn't take long to arrive to that point)—everyone except for me. I was still somewhat blind, or as they say in Narcotics Anonymous, "in denial." I was determined to believe that my status was still up to par, and that I could stop at will. I did know that I wasn't as good of a soldier as when I first arrived.

Whom was I kidding? The drugs were indeed taking hold of me. And no matter how hard I'd try, I couldn't defeat the powerful urge gripping me. Sgt Jones intervened. He made it clear that if I ever needed someone to talk to, he was there. He even gave me insight as to what was being discussed, although he wasn't the only person who showed me they were genuinely concerned about me and my military career.

The addiction left us despondent. The once cared-for home and even the kids were being positioned to the rear of our list of things to do. Getting high was quickly moving into the forefront of our lives.

We were failing miserably as parents and forsaking all responsibility. All we began to think of was the high we'd receive once my payday came around.

I tried to productively balance the life of using drugs along with the life as a soldier in the United States Army; however, the over-whelming addiction brought on by the cocaine made it impossible. My life was in shambles, and all I could foresee was my next high. "How did it happen so fast?" I often asked myself. The colonel had done everything in his power to assist me in receiving treatment. Without question, he and the command sergeant-major cared about the transformation my life was taking.

"What can we do?" they each asked.

"I need help, sir," trembling as I forced the words from my mouth, tasting the salt from the tears my eyes had released. I knew their patience was running thin with my neglect. Instead of being at my appointed post, ready for duty, I would be in Laurel, Maryland or Washington, DC chasing the dope man in hopes of discovering the 'working half,' they called it, the rock of cocaine.

I had been smoking cocaine for approximately three months now, and my secret was out of the bag. Upon discovering the hidden secret of my drug addiction, the colonel clarified that it would be a good idea if I went to see the post psychologist. "I don't understand why I need to see a psychologist, sir," I replied, "My problem is drugs." But it was true, some of my issues did stem from a psychological disorder, some thought process I had yet learned to master.

If I could have looked into my eyes, I would have clearly seen that the mere fact I was renting out my new car for drugs would have brought me into agreement with everyone else. But to the persons caught up in the addiction, I have learned that seeing clearly is impossible.

Having my vehicle rented out for dope most of the time left me searching to find my own way from point A to point B. I quickly grew tired of walking, and coming up with a grandstand idea, suggested to my Puerto Rican partner that we should borrow someone else's car for a short while. (I guess if the person doesn't know you're borrowing it, then it's considered stealing, huh?)

I was sinking further and further into a destitute state. My mental capacity appeared to be growing short and quick tempered from the long nights and lack of rest. We constantly ran from city to city, getting from one place to another as best we could when my car was in the possession of the Jamaicans. I was losing massive weight. And my body began to feel broken and weary from entertaining days of vigorous running. We both were completely exhausted after returning from our journey. I entered the apartment, collapsed onto the sofa, and within seconds had blacked out. I had been out for hours, I was told by my wife. I noticed when I had regained conscientiousness, that my wife was holding a pack of ice cubes behind my neck. She stated the cold ice would help revitalize me. I guess she knew that little trick from experience, I imagined.

My world had become a nightmare filled with lies, depression, and anger. Everyone who had faith in me now feared even having me in their presence. The colonel had relieved me of duty some time ago. My failure to show up for formation and my unresponsiveness to their phone calls, lead them to believe that I had gone AWOL (absent without leave).

Whenever I was granted an occasional break from getting high, I would often sit in front of a huge wood-trimmed mirror located in our bedroom and glance at my disfigurement induced from the active participation of drugs and alcohol. It was a sad, sad sight to gaze upon. The reality that I was truly a crack addict finally set in. No longer was I able to lie to the man in the mirror. It was obvious to everyone, and now it was even obvious to me. I could do no more denying. Looking at the man in the mirror, I cried. Motionless, I stassred at the thin face that once held a display of fullness.

My wife was completely oblivious to my emotional state and the tears I'd cry in my secret place. Silently, crying out in anguish and despair, I'd attempt to conjure up enough faith that could halfway give me some relief. I hoped that the God of whom Mom spoke with such confidence would rescue me from the *hell* I was now living in. "If you're real, God, I need you desperately," squeezing out the words as I watched my face fade into the abyss of my mirror.

I elaborated constantly to my wife of how my life was prior to meeting her. I tried hard to convince myself that "if it hadn't been for her, I wouldn't be in this mess." The blame had to go to someone, I suppose. "After all," I said, "you are the one who introduced me to cocaine in rock form." But the truth of the matter was, I was already getting high; and I wondered how long would it have taken before I had found my own way to crack cocaine? But she was the nearest target, and the one responsible—no one else, I concluded.

I asked God, "Why is this happening to me? Have I done something so terrible that vengeance upon me was now being served?" I needed some answers. My life was slipping away. And things grew worse before they grew better.

My drug habit increased far beyond controlling. Members of my unit would come by my apartment as always, hoping to catch me at a point of rest. They could never sneak up on me because I always made sure I could see anyone approaching my building through a peephole cut out from my living-room curtain. And if by chance I missed them, allowing them to gain access to my door, I'd dismiss the knocks as if it was just my imagination playing tricks on me. But they were persistent. The officers were determined to gain entrance into my home to arrest me and take me back to the military base where I would be placed on restriction until my hearing for discharge or jail.

The crack binges spiraled so far out of control that they sent me fleeing Fort Meade, Maryland. In the process of our reckless journey, we had driven another stolen car to Brooklyn, New York, the Flatbush area where we knew undoubtedly that we could sell it. The second car would follow us closely behind in either a rental or someone's own personal vehicle that carried another group of people who either chose to go along for the ride, or who simply wanted to purchase some drugs of their own in hopes of sellling back in Maryland for a hefty profit. It wasn't hard to exchange the vehicle for the capsules of crack cocaine and the ounces of marijuana. This surely wasn't our first trip to the area.

Everyone agreed that once we "copped" what we were looking for, it would be best if we hid the capsules of crack inside the tire, and the marijuana in the engine. The decision was unanimous. Tony handled the transaction. I rode with him to Brooklyn, but he handled the transaction.

We were excited about our purchase! Everyone claimed first dibs from the homemade crack pipe or can. We couldn't wait to get out of Brooklyn. But in the interim of trying, we accidentally made a wrong turn, and somehow ended up heading toward the Bronx. I had never been to the Bronx, and from the war stories I heard, really had no intentions of going.

The party began as quickly as we entered the car. No one was about to take a hit first, Tony and I both agreed. We were determined that, since we were the ones who did all of the dirty work, we should receive first dibs on the "pleasure pipe." Really, it didn't matter, because these weren't your amateur crack smokers; everyone had their own tool for getting high.

We were headed down I-95 south, enroute to Fort Meade, Maryland, enjoying the sounds of music blasting, along with each person smoking until their heart's content. Someone noticed a State Highway Patrol tailing us. The flashing lights coming from nowhere. Instantly and in a consecutive motion, my heart gave way to a pounding I never thought existed.

I knew what would happen to me if I was arrested for the possession of drugs. An eerie feeling came over me, and suddenly, the good time I believed to have been having was cut short. All I could think of now was how many years I would receive in the prison called

Fort Leavenworth. My heart rate accelerated faster at each thought of being sent to prison; I surely wasn't ready for that.

I knew that the Army would convict me if I was found with drugs while still under active-duty status. My discharge hadn't come into effect, yet. Therefore, by all legal rights, I was still classified as an active-duty soldier. That meant all the difference in the world. I was terrified.

Everyone in the car must have been feeling the same way, because as soon as the police officer made his way toward our vehicle, just like canaries singing their most melodic tune, everyone began to say that they were **not** going to take the rap. Everyone was content to smoke and drink, but as soon as the trouble came our way, all friendship was gone; it was every man for himself.

I started the whole thing off by saying, "I can't take the fall for this. You guys know what will happen to me if I get arrested for this stuff." From the expression on everyone's face, it was clear they, too, felt the same way about what would happen to them if they were convicted of trafficking. Nobody wanted to take the blame for that. They weren't about to let me get off scot-free, especially since I had gone with Tony to "cop."

The officer approached our car swiftly. His right hand was resting on the handle of his weapon, appearing ready for whatever came his way.

Everyone tried as smoothly as they knew how to conceal the paraphernalia. Some even attempted to slide it in the direction of the next man to pass the blame on him. This group was scandalous.

The officer's first stop was to the driver-side window. As normal police protocol called for, he asked the driver, the mother of Tony's eight-month-old daughter, for her license. Then, as if there was a remote control attached to him giving specific instructions as to what to do, without any hesitation he asked, "Is there anyone in the car currently in the military?" He further stated, "If there is, you know what's going to happen to you; you're looking at twenty years of hard labor."

I wasn't sure how much time I would be facing or if his statement was even true, but I wasn't about to leave it to chance. "I'm not about to do anybody's twenty-five years of nothing," I thought. One by one, he began to excuse us from the car, motioning towards the rear. He said that he would provide us a chance to make a confession and that his only concern was for the individual who purchased the drugs; everyone else would go free. No one believed him. He kept persisting that we make a confession or everyone in the car was going to jail, including Tony's eight-month-old baby girl who would be taken to New York Child and Family Services. We fought back and forth deciding who would be the sacrificial lamb. It was stupid of us to drag a newborn infant along with us on a drug purchase in the first place, but thinking as dope fiends, we had thought it would provide for us a better disguise.

The officer insisted we tell him who purchased the drugs. We saw that he was running out of patience with us. "All I want is the buyer," he said. There were probably 300 capsules of crack hidden inside the tires and four ounces of marijuana stashed away in a compartment near the engine.

As one person stood outside with the officer, pleading his or her case of not being the individual responsible for the purchase and denying that there were any drugs inside the car at all, the others remained inside the car fighting amongst each other until their turn. I'm sure the policeman could hear the arguing. Each person adamantly proclaimed that he or she wasn't about to take the fall for something they hadn't done. It became an all-out, divided war.

Before it was my time to exit the car to undergo my pat-down and questioning, I said a lengthy prayer asking God, "Please don't let me go to jail." I remembered seeing some of my prayers answered in the past and, although I wasn't a student of the Bible nor considered myself a devout Christian, I did believe in God. I felt I had no other alternative; God would have to be my only way out of the mess. I prayed like I had never prayed before, while everyone else was arguing back and forth. I was silent, in fear for my life, which could possibly be snatched away in a twinkle of an eye.

My wife stared at me intently, reading my fear through the love she shared for me. She would have done anything for me, I believed, even if worse came to worst, taking the rap for me. I prayed that would never be the case, that neither of us would receive jail time. The thought of leaving the kids crushed me. "I hadn't even spent time with them," I thought to myself. Every thought imaginable was running through my mind. I was worried that this might be my last day of freedom; that is, unless the officer learned who purchased the heavy quantity of drugs.

"Oh, God, please don't let me go to jail!" offering my most sincere prayer ever prayed. "If you get me out of this, I promise to serve you! I promise I will change my life!" I gave everything I had in me to give. When it finally came my turn to receive my informal interrogation, I admitted to the officer that I was presently in the United States Army, stationed at Fort Meade, Maryland. He recited the words he had stated upon his initial approach, clarifying now in more detail my outcome if I was found to be the person responsible for the purchase.

"Yes, sir, I completely understand," I said.

"All you have to do is tell me who copped, and you're off the hook," he said, attempting to strike a deal with me.

It wasn't a bad deal at the moment, I thought, and gave it great consideration. "Let me discuss it with the others," I said.

"All right," he replied, "but you all have only five minutes to tell me what I want to know, or everyone's getting arrested … and the child … well, you know where she's going to end up."

It was nice of him to permit us to talk it over. Our whole aim was to convince the person responsible to "'fess up," as we say. In actuality, Tony was the purchaser; I was just there for the ride. He wasn't accepting any of that wacked-out suggestion. Before he'd do that, he'd pin the deal on the mother of his child.

The officer's ultimatum had us physically ready to come to blows with each other. Everyone came up with all sorts of excuses as to why he or she couldn't take the blame. But no one's excuse was as good as mine, I figured, and my wife agreed. We had recently gotten married, and she didn't want her family to be torn apart over some person not willing to 'fess up to what they had done. She wasn't about to let that go down, to paraphrase her actual words.

The police officer's patience had run out, putting more pressure on us to "drop the dime" on the person responsible. It was unanimous. "He did it!" we all agreed. A lot of us were upset with him, because he had cold-heartedly told the officer that the mother of his child was the person responsible. That didn't set well with any of us. The fact that he could stoop so low as to send the mother of his newborn daughter to prison for a long time told us that we had justification in turning the table on   him. Besides, he really was the purchaser.

The officer gave one final attempt at allowing us to resolve our own issues, once again calling me out of the car for questioning, believing, I suppose that I would be the weakest link simply because of what I had to lose. For the second time, he patted me down. My nerves were frazzled, hoping and praying that he didn't discover the fifty capsules of crack I had hidden in my underpants. There was no doubt in my mind who was about to be extracted from the group.

When I re-entered the car, grateful that my prayer had been answered, I swore to my wife that we were about to stop this foolishness and start going to church, immediately upon arrival! The officer had arrested the purchaser, and everyone believed they had done the right thing.

I knew I had an obligation to fulfill, I reminded myself. But right now, I said, feaning for a hit of the crack pipe, "I need a hit." At this very moment, all I could imagine was taking a hit of dope with hopes it would calm my nerves. I knew it was nothing but the Lord sheltering me. Not allowing the officer to find the vials of crack on me was nothing short of His Grace—that, I knew enough about. And just as I had promised, I truly was going to change my life. But for now, I needed a hit of crack badly.

The whole car had just gone through a metamorphosis. Dim looks were on all of their faces, as if the Grim Reaper had come and stolen the life of their best friend. But I don't believe that was the case at all for the sad display. Nah, truthfully, I believe it was because there wasn't any more smoke product. As far as they knew all of the crack was recovered by the officer. I liked the secret I had, feeling as if I was now the controller! According to their knowledge, no one in the car had anything to smoke on our voyage back to Maryland.

The travel seemed long, mainly because everyone's spirit was low. No one wanted Tony to go to jail. As we approached our destination, seeing the bridge that would carry us back over to Baltimore, everyone's spirit livened up. Everyone was filled with the aspiration at the fact that all of us except for one individual had not ended up in jail. I knew that once they learned that I still had many capsules of crack vials on me, their spirits would really light up. I couldn't contain the secret any longer. All the way home I wanted to burst from trying to contain my secret. I wanted to smoke just as bad as the next man, so for me to hold out until we got out of New Yor, and the other states was more than I could bear. But as soon as we hit Maryland, "It was on!"

I revealed my secret first to my wife. Then, as I shared with the others, they joined me in believing that this was justification for a real celebration, a celebration that would begin the greatest smoke fest known to man!

"It's merited," we said, "After what we just went through, we deserve it!"

"I have the right to go first," I said. "After all, if it wasn't for me ..."

They agreed, but in their hearts, I was certain, neither of them wanted to comply.

I hadn't responded to any of my commander's messages left on the answering machine and feared the repercussion. My commander had clearly stated that I would be brought up on charges if I didn't respond within twenty-four hours. I took that as another justification to continue our party. This time, I believed it would be best if we left base and head for Southeast DC to a mutual friend's house.

I never responded to the allotted time frame the post commander issued. A warrant for my arrest was issued again. And for the second time, I was listed as AWOL. This meant big trouble, trouble I really wasn't sure I could handle.

The concern for my whereabouts sparked a lot of interest, and with my failure to comply with the commander's order on this occasion, my mother was contacted in belief that I may have returned home. Word had spread back in my hometown that I was missing. And my mom, as I was told later, "Gave me over to God."

For several days we traveled back and forth, buying and smoking cocaine, leaving the kids with either my wife's brother or even sometimes with other folks. But rarely did we leave Chastity with anyone; we often carried her along with us. Caught in a living hell, I continued to submerge deeper.

I discovered a letter—actually not a letter at all, but the promised warrant for my arrest, and an attachment letter that stated, "Turn yourself in at once." I was afraid, deeply afraid. Everything I had worked for was about to come to an end. My behavior had deteriorated from bad to worse, and my life was floating on a continual down-hill slope without any brakes. Things had to change, I very much knew, but the addiction wouldn't allow me.

I reached for the Bible that sat on top of the coffee table. It hadn't been read for quite some time by either of us. I knew I'd gain some comfort by reading it. I always did, if only for a moment's worth. Gracefully, I retrieved it, flipped through the pages carefully, searching for the only scripture I felt connected to, Psalm's 23, and stared upon the words Mom quoted, "The Lord is my shepherd …"

Uncertain as always as to the meaning of the verse, I continued reading. I knew Mom gave me that scripture for some reason or another and I was searching to find the answer. Consequently, she had given this Bible verse to me before I left for boot camp. Also, she ended all of her letters with this scripture. Therefore, I believed even more that this scripture truly contained value and importance.

Despondently, I closed the Bible; and, having difficulty placing one foot in front of the other as I walked away in shame, I retreated into my bedroom in search of but a single moment of clarity. Robotically, I flopped down in the chair that faced the lengthy mirror. This was my place of confession to myself, and something of mumbled words came forth. I noticed my lips moving, but the words were unclear.

The reflection in the mirror displayed itself as an image of death. I was worse than in the few months that passed when I first sat and observed myself in the mirror. I wasn't the man I once knew. There was a huge problem. In despair, I reached into the bottom right-hand drawer, where we kept a stolen police .357 Smith & Wesson pistol. Without the slightest hesitation, I raised the gun to my right-side temple and hoped that once I pulled the trigger, I would feel no more pain, that it would be all over, and that I wouldn't have to suffer anymore.

I was unable to hold back the tears I shed in the process of wanting to commit suicide. I prayed that God would forgive me for what I was about to do, but I had had enough. Now I was determined to take matters into my own hands. God was taking entirely too long, I concluded.

"Did I really want to commit suicide?" I asked myself. "Was suicide really the answer?" I was tormented. On one hand, I wanted to end it all, but on the other hand I desperately wanted to live. A sermon that a preacher had preached entered the spiritual war: *if you commit suicide, you will go to hell.* I heard it clearly, as if God Himself had spoken that audible message that made me surrender the .357 back to its original place. I feared dying but feared hell even more. I couldn't do it. As bad as my life was, I had to fight to sustain it. I was willing to fight for a second chance at life. I was losing the battle, it seemed, but I decided to fight until I had no more breath.

I could do nothing except drop to my knees. The weight upon me was heavy. I repeated the proposition to God mentioned on the highway of I-95. "If you'll help me Lord, I'll serve you." I struggled to my feet, weary from the loss of energy. Reluctantly, with my right hand I applied a firm grasp to the telephone receiver. In slow motion, I began punching the numbers to Sergeant Jones. I feared the consequences and knew very well that it was going to be a long, dreary process.

I was nervous, yet a little relieved to finally be in communication with Sgt. Jones. He asked if I would like him to come to my house. Once we finished our conversation, I searched the house for my wife, hoping to share the results of my telephone conversation. But as I walked from room to room, already thinking the worst assumptions, I foud that she had slipped out even before I had finished talking.

My sergeant arrived within minutes only to find me a total mess. He was shocked to see me in that condition, and in almost a faint whisper, asked, "What happened?"

What could I possibly say? I knew he was right—I did look a mess. My body was disfigured, and my once masculine figure had shrunk three sizes. Each time I looked in the mirror, death seemed to be the only presence I recognized.

I could see the expression on his face. The apathy in his voice was soothing, but his eyes watered slightly. He remembered this young, vibrant, super-trooper soldier he had first met. Now I was reduced to skin and bones. It hurt him to see me in this condition, I knew, for it was obviously noticeable in his countenance.

We sat for approximately a half hour before he decided it would be best if I got some rest before going to face the colonel and command sergeant-major in the morning. Closing the   door behind him, I could see his disgust and pain. He liked me as a young soldier and would have done anything to help me in my crisis, but I had gone too far. Staying away without calling the command post was forbidden, an irrevocable sin, and I had committed it twice. The first one I lied my way out of, but this time, I had been gone for a few weeks. There was nothing I could say to clear me from the punishment I knew I had to face. Only God could get me out of this one!

I sat alone in my house trying to muster up the right words I would say to my superiors. I was truly scared. My wife hadn't returned. She was somewhere chasing more crack, I suppose. Therefore, I was left all alone to bear the load that no one could help me carry. I needed to speak with her, but the drug was more important than any of my problems.

I sat reading more of the Bible, continuing with the verse in Psalm 23 that I had begun reading before the interruption. Doing my best to pray again, I mumbled words, hoping I was on the right track. My life was in total shambles. All I could do was to sit back on the sofa and reminisce. I reflected on when I was a kid playing football in the street before Mom called for me to come indoors. I reflected on when I was in the church choir. All sorts of scenes began appearing from nowhere as if I was viewing some sort of slide-show presentation of my life. I remembered the years before the drugs came along, mainly the crack, and how even then I still managed to hold on to some kind of Innocence. But now, I was dying and felt my life falling to ruins. My military career, in just a few hours, would be a memory.

In conversation with the Lord, I asked, "What is it you want from me? Why is this happening to me? Do I have a purpose? If there is a purpose for me, then show me." There was no restraining the anger, nor the tears that fell from my face.

In the middle of my questioning God, the door to my apartment opened. It was my wife and two other folks she had found in the streets. "I'm not ready for anymore partying," I said, "I'm in enough trouble as it is." She paid me no attention. As if I hadn't said a word, she introduced her guests. Seductively, she grabbed me by the hand and led me into another room. Working up her nerves to ask me something, she finally asked if she could use my car.

I began telling her of my situation, all the trouble I was facing, and what I was instructed to do in the morning. She didn't care. The only thing on her mind was going to purchase more dope. She pretended to hear me but never ceased to enforce her desire to use the car. We went through an exchange of issues, appearing as if one was attempting to prove that their point was more important than the other's. I told her that I would have to move back to the barracks, and that she and the kids needed to find a new place to live. I told her that she was no longer permitted to live in post housing once I accomplished my visit with the colonel. That did not seem to faze her, at the time. I gave up.

"Here, just come right back." I said. Something told me not to give her the car keys, but I think I wanted her out of my face. She kissed me on the cheek and quickly made her way to the door, followed by the girls that were with her. The house was completely empty once again. The kids were being watched by their aunt and uncle. I didn't have anyone with whom I cared to socialize with at the moment. I needed the solitude.

I must have fallen asleep because I didn't remember her coming into the house. When I had awakened, I noticed she was still awake. I wondered if she had been asleep at all. The day was early, and before I knew it, the military police (MPs) were at my door to escort me to the captain's office. I knew what they wanted, so there was no need for me to play stupid. I was on my way to hear my first court-martial ticket, and my wife couldn't have cared less.

Sergeant Jones accompanied the base police officers. He wanted to do his part in assuring that I received fair handling. We weren't far from my housing unit; therefore, the trip was short. Once reaching the barracks where the brigade captain's office was, the sergeant took control and escorted me into the unit where I would face the first person in command, Captain Burns. I'll never forget the stares as I made my way inside. Most had not seen me in quite a while and were shocked at the results. I was completely unrecognizable, and my military uniform was even baggier than before. By this time, I had lost nearly thirty pounds. My face was disfigured; not even a belt couldn't keep my pants from sagging. My gaunt appearance was indeed noticeable to everyone, especially those who had known me prior to my severe addiction. There was much sympathy shown towards me by my peers, and many said that they would pray for me.

The Captain was very brief and to the point in his reprimand, mostly mentioning how I could possibly receive jail time for my actions; however, "it's up to the brigade colonel to make that decision," he said. "For now, he said, you are placed on barracks restriction until further notice."

"I knew that was going to happen," I said to myself. And if truth were to be told, I was glad that it happened that way. Part of me wanted desperately to break away from my wife and the destructive lifestyle i n w h i c h we were engaged. This would offer me some sorely needed, long overdue rest. I really couldn't be angry at my commander, I considered. In actuality, he was being used to save my life. I rested in the bed of my old room, with my old roommate, the guy from Florida. The night's sleep was the best I had received in a long time.

The next day was a day I was painfully regretting to see. I sat on standby waiting to receive my orders to go to the Brigade Building. It was guaranteed that this would be the finality of my once prosperous military career. It seemed like my entire life constituted prayer. Every situation I found myself in warranted me to talk to God. I stayed in a bunch of messed-up situations, one after another. I was in trouble.

If I had any other kind of prayer up my sleeve, I had best begin to recite it now and hope for the same results, I thought. This was my final fate, possibly hard time in prison; I was a nervous wreck.

The moment I feared had arrived. I heard the orders instructing Private First Class Smith to be escorted to the Brigade Building to see the colonel, at once! The ride, just like before, was quick. I had hoped for more time, believing the distance would calm my nerves. We arrived much too soon. My nerves raced recklessly through each part of my body, and all I could think of was, "What is my wife doing?" I had to gain control, I knew, but doing so wasn't easy.

I made my way into the clearance building, gave my secret- clearance ID badge to the officer working the desk, and at his command proceeded up the stairs where all would rest upon the shoulders of my brigade colonel. I knew he liked me, but I had messed up royally this time. I needed Jesus, for sure, was all I could think!

Once again, piercing stares penetrated my concentration. I tried to go into a zone, blocking out the gossip all around me. I knew I was the talk of the unit—if not the entire base. But it didn't matter anymore, because if the colonel and *God* allowed me to escape this, I was going back to Cincinnati, Ohio where I belonged!

The colonel and the command sergeant-major were expecting me, so there was no need to be announced by their secretary. She told me to go right on in. "They're waiting for you," she said. The door was already ajar when I approached the sergeant-major's office. The colonel was also located in his office for this case. I knocked carefully, but loud enough for them to hear me. Immediately, I was instructed to enter. I stood at attention until further orders to stand at ease, meaning I could relax. The procession began by the colonel rendering me a few fatherly, heartfelt words. And the sergeant-major, who was a wise role model any kid would have loved to have as a father, did the same. They both cared what happened to me. I knew that, but all I could think of right now was hoping to God I didn't go to jail.

After the consultation, it was time for the business at hand to begin. The colonel, leading off the disciplinary procedure, began reading from an arsenal of charges brought against me. *Scared* wasn't the word, by now. The charges carried heavy prison time, if convicted. Where was God, I wondered?

Once the colonel finished reading the complete list of charges, he then moved towards me while still offering words of encouragement and sympathy. I was losing another rank. My actions had already caused me to lose one rank, already. I went from a private first class (PFC), to a private (E-1).

The only thing I would have to show for all the years and hard work I put into the military was an empty uniform collar, I thought, then concluded, "It beats going to jail!" But that wasn't out of the question as of yet, either.

His closing comments were, "Your security clearance has been revoked. Turn in your ID badge at the desk and report back to Captain Burns."

At that point, I was immediately placed on barracks restrictions—indefinitely, this time. Extra duty was also a part of the punishment. And, again, the psychiatrist was mentioned.

After completing several nights in the barracks, I decided it was time for me to go. I called frantically for my wife to come pick me up' after all, she still had my car. Within minutes she was there, and off for DC we went. We didn't waste any time going to our usual dope spot. They all knew us and welcomed us as we entered the scene. This was a tough neighborhood, nothing except dope dealers and gangbangers—serious bangers, not like in Ohio. We were nothing compared to these cats.

While we were in the neighborhood searching for our particular baggy color, we were pulled over by a policeman. Immediately, I assumed it had something to do with my departure from the barracks. I was terrified, but even that's an understatement. I was being pulled over left and right, it seemed, as if it wasn't enough for me what had happened leaving New Yor —one police disaster after another. Had I known the Lord more in depth, I would have recognized that it was He who was speaking.

I was familiar with the routine, by now. As always, the same procedure followed: my driver's license or picture ID. I wanted to run, but reconsidered quickly, knowing I'd be caught and possibly beaten. I did as I was instructed and, after running my name through the computer, he returned and asked me to step out of the vehicle. This time I knew there was no escaping; I was going to jail. It was true; they did have a warrant for my arrest, but for a stolen car. I lost it, "What stolen car?!" I said ticked off. "I don't know nut'n 'bout no stolen car; you must have the wrong person!" They didn't try to explain anything, only telling me to get into the cruiser and be quiet.

I didn't want to make them angry, I knew very well of their reputation, sort of like Cincinnati, Ohio's. I remained silent the entire trip before noticing that we were at the DC jail. I had heard war stories about that place, so I had no excitement about experiencing it through first-hand knowledge. I won't even lie; I was nervous. The gangs were in this place super thick, and I didn't want to cross anybody. But I knew I couldn't go in there acting like a coward, either. I had to be ready to handle my business if a cat got jazzy. I would be forced to stand my ground and knew that I couldn't back up.

They informed me of the actual charges while booking me in at the front desk. I couldn't believe it! The car I had rented for the Jamaicans was considered stolen. I knew they had gone to Brooklyn. I also knew that they were back in Maryland during the time of this arrest. I tried to contact my wife so that she could find them and straighten this matter out. She couldn't be reached, as usual, and was probably glad that she had the car and the house to herself, I imagine. I contacted her brother and he had no idea of her whereabouts, either.

I had rented the car for only one day. But according to the rental company, it was turned in a day later. The warrant was already issued and had never been retracted. The car was on their parking lot. But it didn't matter, I was charged with grand theft auto (GTA), as it's known in the police department. This charge carried three to fifteen years of prison, if convicted. I would be held in the district jail facing the charge, until the matter got straightened out.

It didn't take long before the Army got word that I was in custody. Soon, they were in the DC jail looking at me through the glass. They basically wanted to know if I had done what I was being accused of, and if I had any knowledge pertaining to the break-ins that were occurring around the base.

I hadn't heard anything from my wife. But, again, I wasn't surprised. I guess she was out having a good time. She loved it when I wasn't around. I couldn't control the thoughts racing through my head. I was worried that my situation with the military might not be too favorable this time. I had no right to leave the barracks; I was still on restriction. I made up my mind to recline on the issued rack. In a sunken state of depression gripping me, I decided to make the big step of going to the telephone to call Mom. I had enough; it was time for me to go home—if I made it out safely.

I was ready to leave the military and further came to the conclusion that if I was to get my life intact, I couldn't be anywhere near

Mina. I also determined that If she was to get her life together, she couldn't be with me. It was a must that we separate, if we stood any chance of having a life with or without each other. We had gone through entirely too much to even think of reconciling. The walls of trust had been completely destroyed. There was deception on both parts. The verbal and physical abuse had reached an all-time high. I swore I would never hit a lady, but she had awakened any beast that possibly lay dormant. I wasn't exempt from hitting women, just chose not to as I grew older. Besides, I never wanted to inflict upon women the same torture I had heard inflicted upon my own mother.

Truthfully, I believe what really told me that it wasn't going to work between us is when we were arguing over some crack, as usual, and the argument turned violent. Before I knew it, I hit her in the Adam's apple with a martial-arts knife hand. The force from the blow closed her windpipe. Hysterically, not knowing what I should do, I began administering CPR. It was by the grace of God she regained conscience. We apologized to each other, afterwards, as if nothing occurred. After giving each other a warm embrace, we began smoking the remainder of our dope. How sick can you get?

The rack was hard. The metal springs popped out through the thin mattress, making it impossible to receive any pleasant night's sleep. I remember complaining. Early the next morning, I decided it would be best to call Mom, this time to see if she would send me some Greyhound bus fare. This wasn't a happy feeling. Uncertain if I was doing the right thing, I dialed the numbers reluctantly, just as I had done when it was time to face the music of the brigade colonel. The phone rang for a while before she answered. Upon hearing her voice, I began to silently cry. It was like something magical came from her. I was careful to only let a few tears make their way from my tear ducts. I didn't care to let anyone see me in my vulnerable state.

As always, the first thing that came out of her mouth was a slew of questions. Naturally, I responded falsely to most of them, as any practicing addict would do. We talked for the allotted time before the phone went dead. However, I was careful to remind her of my need for a bus ticket to come home.

She had no idea that there were folks out there who wanted to do bodily harm to her baby, "her number seven." It was imperative that if the Army released me from active duty, I make my way straight to Cincinnati, nonstop! I had messed up a lot of money, and they wanted some form of payment. I thought everything would be all right if I could just get back home. I was certain the environment would do me a world of good. But as it stood right now, I had way too many issues clinging and haunting me in DC and Brooklyn, New York.

But for now, my biggest problem was the military. I believed they wanted blood this time. After I beat the case for grand theft auto (GTA), they'd have nothing on me and would have to release me. But I wouldn't be out of the fire yet. I still would have to return to base and fight the other wildfire I had started. All I could do was to hang my head in the palm of my hands and do as I had been doing for quite some time now — cry. Life was miserable.

Within two weeks, I knew it should have been my time to leave. There was nothing giving the jail cause to keep me. I said, "The car has been returned." confirming my innocence to another prisoner, like he even cared. It was two weeks too long since I entered the district jail. And now that I was in my third week of incarceration, I grew mad at the world for keeping me locked up for a case I knew I hadn't committed. I was rotting away in a jail and not once had my wife come to visit. Then out of nowhere she showed up, giving me some lame excuse for not being able to come sooner.

She was the last person I cared to see. Broken as I was, she could offer no words of inspiration to sooth me. But why should I have expected anything different? I asked myself. I knew what she had been in the streets doing, so really there was no need for me to expect anything. I did not inform her of my conversation with my mother and my plans to return to Cincinnati—without her.

My thirtieth day came before they finally announced I was free to go! I couldn't wait to get out of there, and even if I still had to deal with the commander, I was one step closer, I told myself. My first call was to my wife's brother. I asked if she was there and if he had seen or knew of her whereabouts. "No," he replied, "But if I see her I'll give her the message."

"Okay," I said. I slammed the receiver on the hook furiously, because that meant I had to walk back to Maryland, which was at least a two-hour stroll. I told myself, "I'm gonna kill her when I catch up with her!"

When I was finally released, the first direction I headed for was to the nearest pony keg to purchase a cold beer. I also knew several other dope smokers that lived near the area, so my first instinct was to go there, hoping I might find her. Then I would personally kill her for making me walk home. Just my luck, she wasn't there. The walk to Maryland meant I would have to use the Baltimore-DC beltway, where there was always a lot of traffic. "But what am I going to do?" I asked myself, "I have to get back to base. And besides, they know I'm released and are expecting me."

It did take me every bit of two or maybe even three hours to reach base. Suddenly, when I decided to take a shortcut, passing the normal hotels we often used as a smoke spot, I noticed my car in the parking lot. I immediately turned boiling red. My heart began to accelerate, and the thought of physically abusing her was about to become a reality. I was determined to hurt her and anyone that was in the hotel room with her.

I rushed to the door and knocked as if I was a police officer. No one answered immediately, so I knocked even harder the second time. Suddenly the curtains rolled back and there she was, half dressed. She had not heard of my release from the District, therefore, my standing at the door was a complete surprise. I heard a man's voice inside the room, and that really made me reckless. She tried to prolong opening the door and my patience had reached its limit. Boom! was the sound of the door that now hung from its hinges. I was correct; there was a man inside the room with her; and just as I suspected, they were smoking dope. "Hola, Papi," she had the nerve to say to me. I was filled with anger I never experienced before. Smoke was everywhere and pieces of crack still remained in the pipe, as if she planted it there specifically for me, believing it would calm me down and make me forget that she was in a hotel room getting high with another man. "Here," she said, "I'm glad you're home." I wanted to take a hit off the crack pipe. All I could think about was the sensation. She knew it, all I needed was a hit, and anything that happened between them would have been quickly forgotten.

Personally, I didn't care anymore. I was leaving for Cincinnati in a couple of weeks, I thought, to myself, so why not join in on the smoke fest?" I could now roam as I pleased since my car was back in my possession.

After the dope was all gone and I had made preparations to take the gentleman back to his community, my wife and I thought it would be good for us to go home and talk about our future together, or if we even had a future. Arriving home, ready to finally relax but knowing from previous experiences that that would be almost impossible to do, relaxing was completely out of the question. The discussion would have to be put on hold, we agreed, until we finished our rendezvous. Back to DC we went, in search of the crack rock.

We were out of money. Then I remembered that Mom had sent me some money through Western Union for the purchase of my bus ticket home. My plans were to get the money and go directly home— without my wife, that is. But I knew I couldn't go anywhere until I learned of my fate with the military.

I showed the proper photo ID to the lady working the window. Without any problems or fuss she handed me the money, minus the company's usual percentage. We were off to the hotel where we assumed we could have some quality time with each other and a peace of mind away from the kids. My plans to use the money for my bus ticket home had vanished. I knew I wanted to go home as soon as possible, but the ultimate decision rested in the hands of Uncle Sam.

The hotel room cost me twenty-five dollars, and I could see why. This was the neighborhood smokers' motel. Yet it would suffice for our purpose, we thought. It wasn't long before my wife suggested using the car again. This was her favorite pastime. We needed some more dope, and I didn't like going outdoors after I had taken a hit of the crack pipe. She knew that and played it to her advantage.

I noticed the time was getting late and still no sign of my wife. Admittingly, I became concerned that I hadn't heard from her. I didn't know she had gone to her brother's house to pick up my baby girl Chastity. The time continued to pass before I decided to go look for her. Walking through the neighborhood, I knew I stood a good chance of being robbed. It was dark, and I knew what could happen to me if I was to walk through the wrong part of town.

Way off, I could see the flickering lights of police cars and some fire trucks. I didn't think much of it at the time when all of sudden a voice inside of me instructed me to turn around. "That's my car!" I said to myself. I punched the accelerator of my two feet and before I knew it I was at the scene of the accident. My assumptions were correct; that was my car. I hadn't noticed at first that my baby girl was also in the car. But after arriving and urgently running to the badly banged up car, I could see that Chastity had been hurt pretty bad. I noticed, also, that my wife had damages ranging from several of her teeth being knocked out to minor cuts and bruises from the impact. Chastity, I was told, had incurred a broken leg and minor cuts. The car was in shambles. Nevertheless, I was able to muster up enough sobriety to give praise to God for sparing their lives.

The officers informed me as to which hospital they were taking them, after learning that I was her husband. I didn't know what to do. Helplessly I plopped down on the nearby curb, thinking how much turmoil my life was in. "What can I do for my wife and daughter?" I thought. I was more determined than ever to make a change in my life.

This had gone too far. Sadness and dripping tears wouldn't release me. I wanted to go to the hospital but it was too much for me to bear, at the moment. There was no way I could see my baby girl in the hospital, badly hurt, all because we had wanted to get a quick fix. "No, no, no," I said frantically. I had reached my limit of misery, I said. "It is time for the Army to do something with me, either send me to jail or release me from active duty status, but something has to happen … and fast!" Exhaustion couldn't describe my feelings and hurt couldn't describe my pain. I wanted to go home.

My only means of transportation was completely totaled. This was my very first, brand-new car. I had purchased it brand new off of the Ford dealership lot. But now, it seemed, the only way I'd be getting to Cincinnati was either by bus or by jail. I saw life as a place in which I had no part. I hated life, and the meaning of it proved nothing of what those fake preachers told me it would be. "Where is God?" I said angrily. I was ready for anything the Army threw my way. "How much worse can it get?" I asked myself.

I had no choice but to collect-call my wife's brother to tell him what had just happened to his sister and his niece— and to ask if possibly I could ride with him and his wife to the hospital. I wasn't excited about going. But truthfully, I should have been there way before them. But I felt I needed a hit to help me deal with the trauma.

Between the wait for her brother and sister-in-law to pick me up, I had ample time to reflect on how I managed to use drugs up to this level of addiction. I reflected back on my childhood when it was all fun and games to get high. There were no major consequences or repercussions for the hangovers the next morning. "Be a man," I was told by the OGs. Yet they forgot to tell me the full story of how it became that they now sat in alleyways and empty buildings. They always told me, "It's all in the mind," was their famous phrase. Well, I had come to believe that it wasn't all in the mind; it was in the liquor bottle and the drugs. If where they sat was based on their mental capacity, then I should have seen way back then that their minds were weak. They were homeless and sleeping in abandoned buildings—my mentors, my heroes, my models.

I was mad at my brother Little Man for introducing me to the negative lifestyle; and I was mad at Tim for leaving me to experience life on my own. I was mad at everyone in my family. As far as I was concerned, everyone had their equal share of the blame. But no one was held more accountable than Dad, I thought. I was angry with anyone I knew. It didn't matter if they had any direct responsibility to my current situation or not, I needed to place blame on someone.

My in-laws arrived while I was still in deep thought. The horn scared me, and headlights glared straight in my face. We entered the hospital in minutes, went through the normal procedure of signing in, then received our directions to their room. I hesitated before entering, afraid of the damage I might see. "Hi, Daddy," were Chastity's first words to me. I looked at my wife lying in the bed next to her. There were no words I could say. I was completely speechless.

She was banged up pretty badly and all I could do was stare at her disfigured face. My car had been totaled, but the fact that they were both alive gave me relief. I knew it was over; I couldn't take any more heartache from Mina. Tomorrow, I would turn myself in to the unit commander and face my punishment; this time I was sure of it. My commander had offered me help in the past, but never did I take him up on his offer. I wondered what would happen now, and if his offer still existed?

This was the day of reckoning. My fate lay in the hands of the colonel and command sergeant-major. I was hoping God still had some mercy on me, hoping he would forgive me for the big mess I made of my life. I was scared, as always, knowing this could go either way.

I no longer had any money to return to Cincinnati; therefore, even if I was free to go I would have to call Mom again and explain to her what happened to the money. She would already know I used it to purchase drugs the moment I began trying to explain myself. But I was ready to face her and knew that eventually she would give in.

Like before, I stood before the colonel and sergeant-major terrified, yet this time it was more frightening. This final meeting was to determine my fate—do I go to prison or do I go home?

Entering their office, again standing at attention until instructed to do otherwise, I gazed, hoping to receive some note from either of their facial expressions or body language of what their decisions were pertaining to my misconduct.

"Stand at ease, Private Smith," said the sergeant-major. I was careful to follow the orders, especially since I was in the dark about my future. "Our meeting was to come up with some alternative plan," they told me. "We don't want to send you to jail." That was the good news to me, and inside, I was dancing for joy! "We have two alternatives," I was told. "Either you can stay in the military and receive treatment in Germany, or you can be dismissed from the military with a general under honorable conditions … choice is yours," he said.

I thought, "Choice is mine? I'm going home!" But I didn't allow them to hear me.

So not to appear excited about their conclusion, I paused for a short while, then as if reluctant stated, "I would like to be discharged, sirs." I couldn't believe they had actually voted in my favor, to release me with an honorable discharge! After all the mess I made … there must be a God!

I couldn't wait to inform my wife. But I was considerate in not telling her until she was released from the hospital. I really didn't care to leave the kids behind, but I knew that if our marriage stood any chance of working, we would have to separate. The thing that displeased me most was having to send the kids back to Connecticut. They didn't deserve what my wife and I had brought upon them. How could I find comfort in that, I asked myself?

I called home as soon as I was dismissed, trying my hardest to explain to Mom what had just taken place. I wasn't really sure myself. Nonetheless, I explained it as best I knew how. She was hurt; I could tell by her voice. But after hearing that I needed more money because

I had smoked up the last money she sent, new energy filled her. Her soft-spoken words grew thunderous as she scolded me.

I was told that it would take two weeks before my paperwork would be complete. I didn't care to leave my wife totally in the dark as to my plans; therefore, I thought it would be best if I informed her quickly. This meant her stay in military housing would officially come to an end. No longer would she or the kids have access to the quarters.

We made arrangements to see each other immediately upon her release from the hospital. She'd be released in one day, and I wanted to share with her details of my trial. The night of separation gave me time to carefully choose how I would handle this situation. She knew as well as I that we couldn't go on living the same way, especially involving the kids. That much we both agreed on.

I suspected the few days laid up in the hospital would have to put something on Mina's mind. She had to see that her life, just as mine, was a living hell. Chastity was elated to be out of the hospital. She had suffered a broken leg but was in good spirits. It wasn't going to be easy explaining to the kids the change that was about to take place in their young lives. It didn't make me feel like a man one bit; on the contrary, it made me feel like a complete failure.

My credit cards were completely maxed out. My car was now totaled. My military career was completely over in one week. And to make matters worse, I had lost my secret security clearance, which gave me entrance inside Washington, DC's Pentagon. It was official: I had completely hit rock bottom.

My discharge papers came within a few days. This meant that I was a completely free man!

"I'm free," I said, to my wife over the telephone, "Free, free, free!" My decision was to immediately get on the Greyhound bus, but the other side of me wanted to stay with the kids. After figuring that I had no money except my last military pay, which wouldn't be sufficient for us to live anywhere, we decided to ask her brother if we could stay with him and his wife, just until I got on my feet. He agreed, but specified that it would only be for a short while. "We don't have enough room for all of you," he concluded.

"That's cool," I said, "All I need is a couple of weeks. I'm going back to Cincinnati."

"What about my sister?" he said.

"I need to go and get *my* life together, then if it's God will, we'll reunite."

He didn't like that one bit. He felt I was abandoning the kids and my entire responsibilities.

For the entire week, we tried reading the Bible, hoping that

would bring about a change in our lives. There were seven people living in this one-bedroom apartment, cramped and literally walking on top of one another. My wife's brother and I continued to discuss my future plans. I told him that I believed our marriage had suffered too much to try and reconcile together, that it was best if we parted ways but stayed in touch. I shared how I believed that that would be our best chance of salvaging our relationship.

My wife and I spoke on a regular basis about our individual plans. Finally, we brought the kids into the mix to explain to them what was about to take place. It wasn't easy, just as we suspected, but it was something that needed to be done, we both agreed. Surprisingly, all of them took it better than we had thought. They probably were ready to get away from the chaos we were putting them through. I promised them I would stay in touch and meant every word.

They told me they loved me and hoped to see me again. That brought tears to my eyes as I thought of the pain I must have caused them. I wanted what was best for the kids. I told myself that, "If it's the last thing I do, I'm going to get my life together and see my Puerto Rican babies again!"

Things were good with our marriage before the drugs came along, I remembered. And at each thought of my remembrance came a tear.

I was finally ready to call Mom again, ready to receive the money for my ticket. She said "no," adamantly and mentioned that she no longer trusted me. I pleaded with her to send the money a second time. When she continued saying "no," I asked if she could send it in my wife's sister in-law's name. After giving that suggestion some thought, she said, "Okay, but if you spend it this time, you may as well stay in New York or whereever you are!"

"I promise, this time, I won't spend it; in fact, she can take me personally to the bus station and purchase my ticket."

"Okay, De'Ron, but this is the last time!"

"Love you, Mom."

"Yeah, good-bye."

The money arrived again through Western Union the next day. Once reaching the conclusion to our decision, my wife accepted the fact that I would be leaving without her. I didn't know what to expect from then on, wondering if we would ever see each other again. My mind was filled with all sorts of delusional thinking. Indecisive as to what I was going to do upon my arrival home, the only thing I knew for certain was that I was ready to go home and start my life all over again.

WHAT A BUS RIDE HOME

IN 1990, the bus arrived inside Washington, DC's terminal, and I was ready to begin a new life. They made the announcement for all those going to Cincinnati to board. The moment brought tears to all of our eyes, hoping this wouldn't be the last time we'd see each other. The kids weren't there, not even Chastity. We embraced, each providing a grip to the other as if to say, "I don't want to let you go!" Slowly, I boarded of the stairs of the Greyhound bus, and hesitantly I took a last look at Washington, DC and at my wife standing in the center of the terminal. I waved my final good-bye!

The window seat afforded me the opportunity to gaze. I needed to do nothing except think of a plan. It was important for me to have a plan of action already in place when I arrived, knowing that without one, Dad was going to raise a lot of static about me coming home again and staying under "his roof." I was already discouraged, sad, destitute, and completely tired of life. The only thing I knew for sure was that I wanted to stop using drugs. How would that happen? I had no clue. But I knew I had to start somewhere, and home is where it would be! For now, that was my number one goal.

The drugs had taken away any identity I once knew. The memory of the former man before my military career was as close as I came to discovering who I was. But now even that was gone. The only clear picture I had was of shattered dreams and visions of the disastrous life I was leaving behind. I had been reduced to a hopeless, drug-addicted failure, in my mind. And how was I ever going to face the people in my hometown who knew me prior to my departure to the military? I searched, hoping to find the answer to my question.

Truthfully, I could withstand the verbal blows from the people in my community who needed something to gossip about. But Mom—how could I ever look her in the eyes?

I had accomplished my change. I thought I had applied all of the right principles. It didn't matter how I obtained my manhood; the fact was that I obtained it, or so I thought. I tried to reassure myself that I had done well in life, despite my setback. "I could still become someone great in life," I whispered to myself, while never really awakening from the trance-like state. I was certain I had become a man, you know, just like dear ole Dad. In reality, I did become just like my father. The things I swore never to imitate in him I found myself doing: drinking, smoking, hitting women … I had become the "monster in the other room." But if the essential part of me still existed; if the innocence I once obtained settled somewhere at the base of my soul; if the God of whom Mom spoke with such profound emotions cared enough for a sinner like me to give me one more chance—I was ready!

I swore I would never be like Dad. I hated all that he stood for. Every pain and hurtful memory came to thought during the bus ride home, and I found myself unable to control the landslide of emotions overtaking me. I tried, but the down effect from the drugs wearing off sent me into another realm.

"The blame—whom should I blame? Surely someone was at fault for not preparing me for the world they knew I would have to face one day. Whom do I blame?" I conferred with myself, before hearing the announcement to exit the bus for a break.

We were approaching Cincinnati in a matter of hours, came the announcement. My heart accelerated from the mere thought of facing Mom. Not out of fear, but out of the disappointment I knew I had caused her. What exactly would her expression be? The last time she saw me I was a buffed soldier ready for war. Now I was returning a paper-weight, sunken-faced, 110 pound, next to nothing boy who needed to revisit the breast of his mother. Pleasing Mom was a long time goal of mine, and if that didn't happen, I'd consider myself a failure, for sure. I knew it wouldn't be an easy task, recovery that is, but this was my first step towards sobriety.

There was a sense of fresh hope the new atmosphere provided. A new outlook on life was projected as I stared at downtown Cincinnati. For a short while, despair was gone and thoughts of something good coming forth took precedence.

There was no one at the bus terminal to meet me upon my arrival. And due to the fact that I was returning on unhappy terms, I didn't really care to call anyone. My first choice was to catch the metro.

I knew I would have to catch at least one more bus in order for me to arrive at my parents' home in Madisonville.

The wait was long, or at least it felt as if it was long. But I'm sure it was anxiety. I waited impatiently number 69, the bus that would let me off one block away from my destination. I didn't want anyone to know of my return just yet, determined to remain concealed until I gained a few pounds.

The bus showed up at least five minutes behind schedule, I remember, causing me added frustration. I was already nervous thinking about how I going to be the laughingstock of the community. My ego was shattered. I wasn't the same man who left, and I knew it. "People will talk about me now, for sure," I thought to myself. Even my best friend Mike had begun spreading rumors about me. "Of all people," I said, "I was his best man in his wedding."

The fare to board the bus had changed. Searching through my pockets to make sure I had enough money, I could feel the stares to which I had grown accustomed piercing me, looking as if they had seen the worst crack addict ever. I admit, I did look pretty bad.

Despite their pathetic stares, I proceeded. I disregarded any and all who judged me as a derelict, and proudly took my seat. The embarrassment that sealed what I had already come to suspect was when I went to take my seat next to a gentleman. He quickly moved to another seat. I was humiliated. Never in my life had I experienced such prejudice. "This couldn't be happening to me!" I exclaimed within. I wanted so badly to disguise myself or better yet close my eyes, and when I opened them, things would be different.

The bus ride to my parents' house took longer than the ride from Washington, DC, it seemed. I was in a hurry to get away from the people on the bus, and I couldn't wait another minute.

Finally! Home at last! I didn't know what I was going to say to Mom once I saw her face to face. "Where do I even begin to tell her how sorry I am?" I pondered as I walked my last few steps towards their house. The front porch was in view, here I was, back where it had all begun. Thoughts couldn't release me; my mind raced. All I could see at this point was her disappointment. "Maybe I shouldn't have come …"

A MOTHER'S TEARS

I knocked on the front door. "Maybe she hadn't heard me," I thought. Boom, boom, boom, boom! I hit the door a bit harder this time. It took a while before someone answered. Suddenly, I noticed the screen door gapping open, slowly. I stood there paralyzed, unable to move a muscle or speak. Her first view of me, I knew, made her think she was looking at death. She too was unable to move. She fixed her eyes on my gaunt appearance, then in one motion gave way to the agonizing tears she was struggling to hold back.

I couldn't imagine the thoughts that were going through her mind. She opened the door a bit wider this time, gesturing that I come inside. Quickly I accepted her invitation, and in the same motion went to embrace her. This time it was I who was unable to hold back the tears.

I knew this had to be the beginning of a new life. It wouldn't be easy, I knew very well. Nevertheless, "the first step must begin, now!" I said. I had to learn all over again the things I once knew, the things I had basically taught myself. I literally would have to relearn how to speak positive things into my life, set small goals, and most importantly give an earnest attempt of trying to develop a relationship with God. The only thing that could hinder me from achieving my goal was that I wanted to do things my own way. I hated authority.

Mom did instill in me some good qualities, such a, compassion and the importance of never hitting a woman—that part went directly over my head.

Before I decided to go to bed for the night, Mom and I engaged in a heartfelt discussion. Our conversations always ended with some sort of Bible passage, and this was no exception. I made her a promise, just one of the many promises I made in the past. My exact words to her were, "If it's the last thing I do, Mom, I'll get my life back!" She nodded her head in agreement.

Determination was a quality she admired about me. She knew that I was a fighter, filled with vigor and tenacity. As I made my way upstairs slowly, drained from the bus ride and sleepless nights, I noticed a smile on her face, as if to confirm that she agreed with my statement and was proud to know that I had not thrown in the towel.

We agreed that I would rest for one week or possibly two before trying to seek employment. I had no problem with that suggestion—I was whupped!

She thought it would be good for me to gain a few pounds rather than appear like I was anorexic. She provided the best nursing care one could ask for. Breakfast, scrambled eggs, cereal, you name it, she provided it!

By the third week I was up and feeling like I had just been resurrected. For once there wasn't a drop of alcohol or drugs in my system. It was a long time since I had been sober for two weeks! I felt fresh and lively. My once gaunt appearance had regained most of its original structure. And where my face had sunken, it was now filled with fullness and shape. I was now in position to go look for work.

This wasn't an easy task. Roadblocks of every kind appeared to have been personally created just for me, it seemed. No employer would even give me an interview. I grew frustrated in a matter of weeks because of the hindrances and negative attitudes they projected towards me. But it was my attitude that was in need of adjustment, I learned.

It was difficult stepping into a new area. I found myself many times being stretched beyond comprehension. My comfort zone was already established, and I knew that the road I was about to travel would only be achieved by suffering and tenaciously persevering. The fighter in me had to endure the journey and I was confident that once given the opportunity I would make it.

A new birth had to arrive. Everything I had learned from the streets, along with the monstrous character I obtained, undoubtedly had to be destroyed and replaced with characteristics likened to the individual I one day hoped to become.

Character was essential for the level of accomplishment I dreamed of achieving. Something on the inside kept driving me to press on, even when I felt like I could go no more. The fierce intensity of flashing scenes projecting themselves continually in my mind was a sign of God's way, reassuring me that He was with me and encouraging me to hold on. I pondered why it was that I was able to see my life from a different perspective, as if I was already living that life. I was there.

Church became my first priority. Once I regained my strength, energy, and self-esteem to leave the house. The people remembered me, and those who had heard of my misfortune offered support and prayers. I knew the journey to recovery would be a hard-fought battle, understanding that there were still plenty of OGs in my community who appeared to have lost. I was determined not to allow myself to fall in defeat as they had— and knew even more so that, if I was to have victory over the perils in my life, God was the key.

My first job was working at an optical eyeglass store. The pay wasn't much, but it provided income, income I desperately needed. I was hired to work in the laboratory, making the eyewear and ensuring the precise measurements were correct before dispensing them to our customers. It was exciting work.

I could see the prayers of Mom coming to pass, her once heart-ached soul now receiving mild joy and relief. The nights she cried and worried about how her baby boy was doing in Washington, D.C., out there in the streets, "her number seven child," were over. I gained satisfaction from knowing that she was happy with me.

All I wanted to do was sit at home and watch TBN (Turner Broadcast Network), the religious station that provided all the inspiration one could ask for. I felt as if my life had been restored, and I owed it all to the Lord! I had discovered my very own tool for sobriety and life, I thought. Working, studying the Bible, and attending church regularly, I was complete in my recovery, or so I thought.

Skating was my way of releasing some of the unwanted pressure. Each week, several members from church would make a pact to go. If I didn't go with one of them, I had no problem finding a ride. For six months, I stayed free from alcohol and drugs. But it wasn't alcohol I believed to have been my problem. My problem was cocaine, I told myself. Therefore, I began to take a sip of liquor or drink a beer with the fellas, daily. Never did I drink alcohol in the presence of the individuals from church. I was determined never to use another drug, confident that that was my only problem, not alcohol. "I'll be fine," I said to myself, "as long as I don't use any more cocaine."

This was a special night skating. The music at the skating rink was pumpin'. There were hundreds of folks skating like it was a roller derby, showing off their new techniques and wardrobes. "I'm not about to be excluded!" I told myself. It was mandatory that "I get in where I fit in," as we say. I did exactly that.

After I zoomed around the rink a few times, it was time for an ice cold can of Colt 45 malt liquor. I made my way to the concession stand, but not without fighting through the crowd that was hanging around, scoping each other to see who they could take home for a nightcap. Then there she was, a young, beautiful tenderoney working behind the concession stand! Immediately, I knew I had to have her.

She waited to serve me my cold beer. But little did she know, I had other intentions besides a beer. I noticed her innocence and commitment level upon introduction. My thoughts were that I needed someone like her in my life, and all would be well! I believed I was ready for another relationship, sure that I was completely over the strain of my wife I left back in Maryland. I decided to wait until later to make my move. The drug addiction, I believed, was history and now I could engage in a meaningful relationship. "The alcohol isn't my problem," I said to myself, as always before engaging. I was really trying to psychologically convince myself. "Crack cocaine is the problem," I confirmed. You couldn't have told me back then that alcohol led me to use cocaine … no, no, no! I assured myself for the umpteenth time. I wasn't about to believe that lie.

The night was almost over, and now I thought was the right time to approach the young lady working the concession stand. I was confident in my ability to receive her phone number. As we exchanged our salutations, I asked her name.

"Denise," was her response.

"Hi, Denise, I'm De'Ron," applying the smoothest voice I could muster. The music was too loud, so our conversation had to end rather quickly. I concluded that I would see her at the end of the night, when I was on my way out the door. She agreed.

I kept my promise to meet her at the end of the session. I advanced to the counter; only this time, in the back of my mind, I knew that I had to receive her phone number. I followed through with my plan. Although acting a bit reluctant to release that information. I could tell that it was a ploy, a "hard to get" attempt. I knew I would have to turn up the charm. I didn't think I was losing her, but knew if I hadn't upped my game, I would come across as weak—and that was definitely not me!

She couldn't resist my poise. I won her over in a matter of minutes, it seemed. In the break of our final words, she smiled, exhibiting an angelic radiance that had to be heaven sent. I knew I had to learn more about this girl. Not all of my intentions were good; as one caught up in sick thinking, my lust also played a major role.

This was to be the last song of the night. I rolled around the rink, taking a quick glance in her direction to see if she was paying attention to my moves. She was, and I knew from that point on we'd be in contact with each other!

"There's one thing I forgot," I told her, as I stopped at the concession stand, "What's that?" she replied, "Ya phone number," I said, noticing the familiar smile that sent me floating.

"You better call me," she said.

"I will," I responded with a sarcastic smile on my face that would give her the impression that I wouldn't. "I promise, I'll call," I assured her as I walked towards the exit.

Before we set our first date, I found myself drinking more often. Under the belief that alcohol had no relevance to my problem, I discarded the idea, saying "Alcohol is *not* my problem."

Kickin' it with my homies one night after work from the eyeglass store, and concealing a pocket full of money, deception found its way home. The small voice was telling me that I could go buy a piece of crack and a woman. I wrestled with the thought continually before finally telling the driver to let me out of the car. I lied and said that I was going to my sister's house located at the corner of Madison Road and Whetsel in Madisonville.

It had been at least six months since my last bout with cocaine. The notion that I was over that particular addiction   was my thinking, until now. I played with the entertaining spirit just long enough to lose the battle. I hurried upstairs to see if there was anyone I could find to satisfy the addictive urge to use. It didn't take long. Any individual needing to be found for the purpose of buying drugs could have easily been found within a block or less. I was okay, I told myself. "I can handle this." But the urge grew more intense. I needed the hit I had long waited for. The female accompanying me stared as I ignited the flame. She watched me inhale, and in the same motion held her breath, as if she was the one taking the hit of crack.

I never learned about any triggers or what makes me desire
the drug in the first place. I was using again, deluding my dear mother into believing that I was staying at one of my sisters' houses. My responsibilities were soon declining. I found myself not caring anymore for the job I had obtained. The same cycle was beginning to repeat itself. I knew I had to stop it before it swirled out of control. I never wanted to ride that rollercoaster again, I always said. But I knew that if I didn't immediately put an end to what was about to take place, I would end up in the same predicament.

I really didn't want Mom to discover that I had relapsed. If I were to lose my job, that would have been a sure sign. That first hit held me captive the entire weekend. My sister Lannie urged me to stop and adjust myself.

She knew that unlike some I had no control over the drug, that once I got started, I was a locomotive out of control. My weight would evaporate instantly. My responsible way of thinking would give way to irresponsibility and faulty rationalizing. "I had to bounce back," I told myself.

My once-full pocket of money was quickly empty. The girls who hung around solely for the purpose of getting high moved onward to their next victim. The pattern was here. I couldn't see it in the beginning, but afterwards I saw something.

I didn't know what I was going to tell Mom. "What possible reason could I provide her for why I have no money?" I asked, discouraged. "I can't lose my job," my thought continued. I knew she'd die if she found out I was using again. I wanted to please her, as was always my intent. She was the driving force for my recovery; "I have to make it!" I said, trying hard to encourage myself.

The day came when I would give the girl from the skating rink a call. This time, I wanted to arrange a date to go to the movies and out for a bite to eat. We engaged in a pleasant conversation over the telephone, and I could feel the energy flowing through the receiver, giving me a sense of ease.

Our conversation lasted for hours, it seemed, the softness of her voice not wanting to release me for the night. The hesitation to hang up the phone was noticed by both, each recommending the other to hang up first, just like two teenagers still in high school. She was exciting and bore an innocence I couldn't get out of my mind.

Before hanging up for the night, we set a date for the upcoming weekend. I borrowed my nephew Bam's car for the occasion. I had never been to her part of town, Hamilton, Ohio, a small Mayberryish city, just on the outskirts of Cincinnati. My first impression of this small community was that of the hills of Alabama. I didn't think, for one second, that this little town could offer me anything.

My drinking had escalated again; therefore, it was mandatory for me to stop at the local store near her house to grab something to drink, something sure to give me the confidence I needed. "This occasion called for something strong, something with the potential of getting me as tipsy as I could imagine; this is an event that only Mad Dog 20/20 or Wild Irish Rose could handle," I told myself. I entered the small store that sat off from the road, asked the clerk for directions, and within seconds was cracking the top to that old Irish fighter called Rose!

I arrived at her house located just minutes from where I bought the "confidence juice." By the time I knocked on her front door, I was well buzzed! A few knocks went by before someone came to the door. I wasn't sure if it was her mother or a relative, so I asked, "Is Denise home?" Although her first name was Christine, she went by Denise which was her middle name. The woman that answered the door yelled for Denise to come. "Someone wants you at the door," she said.

"WOW! She looks beautiful!" I said to myself, my mind quickly running toward the gutter.

"Are you ready to have a good time?" I asked.

No words came from her mouth, just a smile. She reached for the door, escorted by me. I assumed that I would demonstrate my gentleman's quality. Then as I opened the car door, there it was, a freshly cut, red rose. She still hadn't noticed the rose awaiting her in the front seat of the car. But as she was stooping to get into the car, it caught her attention! Still there were no words, only that familiar smile. Then, as if my ears were hearing things, "Thank you," she said, in a tone of a whisper. Right then, I knew I had done something impressive.

I enjoyed her company, but it was obvious she carried a shy disposition. I found that to have an excellent appeal. However, I truly believed my true attraction to her was the fact that she had no connection with the street life. I hated females who ran wild in the street. In my mind, I believed they were only good for one thing … But she was pure.

We reached the end of our night outing. We both shared how we enjoyed each other's company and had a wonderful time. It was only right for me to escort her to her door, I thought, the gentleman I was. It would have gone against our gentlemen's code, had I not.

Things rapidly began to increase in our relationship. She hadn't discovered my drug usage at this point, but it was only a matter of time before the lid would blow. The first sign of trouble came when I lost my job in optics as a lab technician. "How could I balance work and the streets?" I asked myself. I knew the answer to the question. There was no way I could.

My drug usage became openly publicized. With compassion, she spoke to me. She made suggestions that at the time I'm sure I didn't care to hear. But she cared about me, this I knew. Unfortunately, I could offer no love in return; at least, not the way she deserved it. I became dependent on her. As much as I attempted to find myself, leaning on her for support was becoming my norm.

The Bible became my sole refuge place, as always. I promised Mom I would never give up that part of my life; therefore, whenever problems arose—that is, issues I had no idea how to handle—somehow, I believed, the Bible would provide some answers. I made many attempts at finding work, and for whatever reason, no one would hire me. I became angrier by the day. The job search was extremely tiresome. The people I encountered at any employment agency or job site acted as if I was a terrible disease. I was fed up! The thought of seeking employment sent angry chills through my entire body. "I know how I can get some money," I told myself. "The streets have everything I need; if nobody wants to hire me, I'll take what I need!"

I really didn't like the life I had come to live again. But what do you do when that's all you know? Still, I hadn't received any justice keeping me from falling back into the lifestyle I abhorred. "That old lifestyle offered nothing!" I said, bitterly, to myself.

As I reflected on where drugs and alcohol had presently led me, I wondered if it was ever meant for me to be anything other than a crackhead and alcoholic. I wondered if God heard me, and would He one day make me into a man? Soon I was at ground zero all over again. The pride I once esteemed so strongly diminished rapidly. The help of police officers and handcuffs sped up the process of spiraling downward.

I had witnessed the insides of many jail cells already. And now, park benches played a huge role in erasing self-centeredness. Often, I'd find myself sitting alone in a neighborhood   park. Everyone associated with the park seemed to have been destitute. My clothes were still fresh; I hadn't succumbed to the place I was when I was in Maryland, but I was declining.

There were many periods of clean times, even if they only came in thirty-day to one-year intervals. There were periods when I abstained from the indulgence of chemicals and narcotics. At times, I went as long as eleven months without using. Then suddenly, out of nowhere, the familiar urge appeared. There were three urges I had to fight, I learned: one urge being the drug addiction; the second being the street life; and the third urge I had to fight was ME! I was my own worst enemy!

My girlfriend paid an ultimate price to be with me. On many nights of noticing that possibly I wasn't coming home, she'd pack up her baby boy Patrick, and head out on search of a rescue mission. I hated when my binges caused her to come into areas that I really didn't care for her to be in. But she loved me, she said, and was willing to help me through my struggle.

I gave every effort to change my life. Yet, I was unable to fully comprehend that there was only one way any real change could occur, as Mom always mentioned. She told me Jesus was the only one who could perform the thing I needed most, that "He is what you've always been searching for." That didn't make any sense to me. I never stopped dreaming of having a better life. It wasn't that I wouldn't work or anything, just that the addiction prohibited me.

Denise was always susceptible to my visions and dreams. She offered nothing but high praises to whatever I said I wanted to become. That characteristic I adored about her. I knew I could count on her. She never demonstrated anything contrary to genuine concern. I hadn't used in three months. Once again, I was fighting to pull myself up from a relapse that had occurred just a few months back.

Certain that I had conquered the terrible disease of addiction for the third time, I decided to start a janitorial company. It was always my dream to be my own boss, promising that I would never work for anyone. I hadn't completely gotten past the point of taking orders, especially with my attitude spinning in rebellion. "Working for someone else, when I could do the same thing that they are doing is out of the question," I told myself.

How could I understand that my issues ran deeper than drugs and alcohol? The mere fact that my terrible thinking played a major role in my destruction was somehow overlooked. For now, the root of all my problems were in the drugs and alcohol, I thought.

Having some clean time under my belt allowed me to work towards the vision of owning my own business. As we say in the streets, "My mind was no longer cloudy." Therefore, it was time for me to show all of the nay-sayers that I could be someone besides a drug addict and alcoholic. I had to prove to them that everything they thought and said about me was about to slap them right in their faces. (We often fall because we're doing things for the wrong reasons. Had I simply recovered for myself, maybe—just maybe—my recovery would have lasted.)

Denise was very instrumental in helping me achieve my dream. At times, after completing an eight-hour shift of her own, she would volunteer to help me clean a few empty apartments of a contract I received. She didn't like the filth, but her loyalty to me and my dream, I believe, was her driving force.

I thought for sure that victory had been reached, and the life I longed to live had arrived. Things were good, I supposed, that is, until I realized that the issues plaguing me ran much deeper than what was evident on the surface. My temper was still uncontrollable. Why? I'm not sure. But I believe today that the motherly affection I looked to receive from Mom became sought out in the direction of Denise. I began looking to her for the affection I never received from my mother, simply put. The sudden anger came out of nowhere. Whenever I felt she offered no caress or intimacy, I became embittered. I still longed to be held in my mother's arms and rocked to sleep or embraced, I guess; in my mind, she provided neither of those qualities. I was a man looking to be loved as if I was a child. It wasn't her responsibility to raise me; it was mine.

My church attendance was a vital contributor in the success of my staying drug free for as long as I had. But my pride would violate any space of humility that I may have thought I had, and once again led me this time even more fiercely back into the world and life of sin.

I rejected repeated offers for help and dismissed many referrals to be admitted into a drug treatment facility. These encounters led me on a six-month crack run. I used money earned from my janitorial service to party instead of building the business. At times, I made anywhere from $1,000 to $1200 a week. That wasn't bad for a new company with limited resources and no reputation. I had more than enough money to party any way I chose but having the mentality that I was some sort of rich tycoon set destruction in motion. I began to completely neglect my girlfriend and the household we were trying to establish. Regularly, I would return home without a penny in my pocket and made up some lame excuse as to why that was so. She believed my lies for the time, never once making intimations that there were any reasons to believe otherwise.

This relapse was worse than any thus far, I thought. This one would place me in overdrive and cause me to engage in things only the devil himself would be a part of. I began a steady stream of robberies and carjackings. But the worst, by far, was the verbal and physical abuse I began to inflict on my girlfriend. I vowed I would never physically harm another female after the scare I received from striking my ex-wife, but I found myself losing all self-control. I would often shed tears of regret after striking her, or possibly just shoving her. The horrific memories of how my dad used to beat my mother displayed themselves in my mind as an image of forgotten poetry. I hated what I was becoming. It didn't matter that my definition of physical abuse consisted of only a push or a grab; the fact that I put my hands on her was inexcusable.

Truthfully, I didn't intend to relive the life I lived in New York and Maryland; therefore, I knew I better do something to deviate from this present course, "But what? And how?" I asked myself. I promised Mom I would change, but "what was I doing back on the road of destruction?" I asked myself. Where is God? I questioned. I was tired; I had been on this drug road for far too long. It was three years since my arrival back to Cincinnati, and I was still battling. "If God is who He said He is, then He best come see about me."

My life was spiraling full-blown out of control again. "How many times can one man rise and fall?" I asked myself with my face covered in tears. "Why can't I get this thing right? I'm tired of living my life this way!" The sorrow was deep. The consequences of my actions were about to catch up with me, and soon—Judgment Day.

Ups And Downs

UP and down was the way of my life. One moment up, the next moment down, reckless and out of control. The great plan of God was about to take place through an intervention by way of a prison sentence for writing bad checks and fictitiously depositing them into an ATM machine. Every deceptive thing I had done was about to receive full payment. The courts gave me ample time to make restitution; but like most dope fiends, we become too caught up in our addictions that we completely neglect any responsibility; our thinking becomes heavily distorted.

Denise was literally going through hell right along with me. After many failed attempts to repay the stolen money the courts, fed up with my negligence, sentenced me to one year in prison. She couldn't take it, she said; "How am I supposed to endure this pregnancy?" I was excited to hear the news about her pregnancy but saddened by my inability to be there to comfort her. "Some changes had to occur in my life!" I told myself for the umpteenth time as I waited in the county jail for my departure to prison.

I understood that I had a new responsibility. I was determined to keep the promise that I made when I was a child, "to be a better father to my son than my dad had been to me." My promise to honor my vow was important and I knew very well that I must maximize all of my eight months in prison.

My spirit wasn't settled from knowing I had hurt so many people. Mom and Dad were first on my list of amends. Then Denise, without question, surely ranked next on that list.

My nights in the county jail were mind boggling, visions of how I lived my life out in the streets, remembering the days when I ran out of money or merchandise, which in turn led me to commit a robbery or carjacking, sometimes with a pistol, sometimes without.

God had become my focus, again. My nights were dedicated to prayer and trying to make amends with those I had caused harm. I was taunted with images of when I sat alone in an alleyway reading my little green pocket Bible, asking God with tears in my eyes to change my life.

I recalled the countless nights of calling my girlfriend, pleading for her to rescue me from some horrific environment. I didn't think of the danger I was putting her in, never imagining at all that those areas didn't care about anyone or anything. I had completely exhausted myself in the streets. They never loved me—the streets, that is. And God knows they never wanted to see me leave. It was a bad marriage and I knew it, but how could I break free?

I knew that prison wasn't a cure for my drug addiction. Nevertheless, I knew that it would allow me time to recuperate and dry out. I had been in the streets for months and as harsh as prison appeared in my mind some part of me was glad to have been heading there. All I could think of was the soon arrival of my son. That meant I would have to change now, for sure. I started my journey of change by going to the jail library to read books on relationships, maturity, how-to books, and biographies. I searched for any answer that could lead me down a course of discovering who I was and what, if any, was my purpose for being here on this earth. All I prayed for were answers. There were no conclusions as to why I couldn't stop using drugs or drinking alcohol. I had this imaginary view of what a relationship consisted of. I contributed my ignorance to my parents' neglect. My obscure viewpoint was the result of projecting disinterest toward Denise. I was looking at what she didn't possess instead of what she did possess. She loved me the way she knew how, and if I had any maturity, I could have seen the "diamond in the rough." I should have nurtured her innocence. "But how could I, when I didn't even know myself?" I said, feeling sorry for everything I had done to her.

Mom, who had come so far from yesteryears, was now an ordained minister. She made sure I always kept Biblical literature, flooding me with cards and inspirational scriptures to help me endure the path I had created for myself. My time was spent conducting bible studies and assisting others with their troubles. Mom told me that I didn't have faith. I thought I did, and surely I believed in Jesus so, I asked myself, "What does she mean, I don't have any faith?" She also stated that I needed to have a "personal relationship" with Him. Again, I thought I did. Behind the wire fence of the minimum camp was a totally different world. I didn't know how I would adapt to a controlled environment. Then, in an instant, I remembered my military training and occurrences that God had delivered me through in the past. It was imperative for me to reflect on a situation that He had brought me through. Remembering what He already done in the past provided strength and faith to press forward.

Sundays at the prison involved ministers from the outside coming to share a few sermons, hoping their message would heal some wounded soul. I found out that every minister or layperson coming in to minister all felt that we needed ministering to more than they. Week after week, different churches came to offer the one-day, one-hour sermon. I'm sure each felt as if they had completed a noteworthy task for God. Most of the churches were pretty good, I'll admit. Then, there were others I wished would have stayed home.

For the most part, everyone brought the same message, how God did this or did that for them! The majority of them testified how God brought them to the place in their lives where we saw them today. It did inspire me. Their testimonies inserted hope from a biblical perspective of God's faithfulness that I never received before. "I'm fresh in my sentence; I need all the encouragement I could receive!" I told myself.

I saw myself standing behind the podium, delivering a similar message that would also bring hope and inspiration to hurting people. I knew I could be good at it! After all, my heart truly was filled with compassion—that is, when I wasn't on crack.

One night while lying on my rack, I unconsciously announced, "I can write a book about my life." Never did I intend on making that statement literal. My desire to change my life was sincere. I wanted to live differently and wanted to never again have anything to do with drugs or alcohol. I meant every promise to God and would pay every vow I made, even if it killed me in the process. I was determined to live my life right, this time, when I got released. I devoted my time to reading, praying and fasting. I truly believed I was becoming a new person, and others said they completely saw the change. Despite all I had gone through thus far, there was still a feeling inside of me assuring myself that, everything would be all right. I was a fighter and determined to win! Part of me found thrill in the challenge. I was always a big dreamer, and this to me was "nothing more than another chapter in my book," I said, being sarcastic.

The months came and went; it appeared overnight. My prison sentence for passing bad checks was near completion— two months, to be exact. I was only days away from starting prerelease, a phase you go through before your actual release date. This phase is meant to equip individuals with the necessary information to ensure their success out in the real world. Soon, I would be tested on everything I had learned, and my confidence level was at an all-time high.

My release date fell just two weeks shy of my son's birth. I knew that could have only happened by way of Almighty God; His perfect timing didn't go unnoticed. I considered the fact that there had to be a divine intervention orchestrating the timing of my release and the birth of my son; my faith grew stronger.

I knew Mom was anxious to see me again. Despite all the pain I put her through, I was still her baby boy; her number seven child, and nothing I had done could take that love away, I knew very well. Accompanying her was a Caucasian girl named Valerie. I only had the opportunity of speaking with her over the telephone. From what my mom told me about her, she was quite an individual, a person who had a genuine heart of giving.

Valerie had become fond of my mother in a mother- daughter way, and my mother likewise. It blew me away how they met. But that wasn't important, I thought. The main importance was that

Valerie was willing to give God a chance at turning her life around. She too, like many of us, was fighting a spiritual battle.

Mom had received her ordination as a minister and had accepted the call to take her under her wings. In my book, Valerie had already gained points with me just by the fact she cared about my mother. I had done many things to try to make my mother proud, so to have someone else involved who shared the same interest really gave me much more relief. Immediately, I accepted her into the family, despite the fact she was a female Caucasian.

April 21, 1994 was the day I felt like I had risen from the grave! I gave Mom a tight embrace upon greeting her and Valerie on the other side of the barbed-wire fence. The anxiety of being free brought forth tears, some because of missing her—nevertheless, I cried.

I dazed out the window of the car, while listening to gospel music playing in the tape deck. The desire to do the right thing was sincere and I was determined to make every effort in doing so. I specifically asked God to guide me and use me in the manner He had used others who came into the prison. My heart was now pure, I presumed. The motives behind my desire were of good intent. I felt I had made a significant change in my attitude and believed that my understanding of life had matured.

When I returned home everyone offered their support, steadily repeating how they hoped I no longer went in the direction of using drugs again. I promised that that phase of my life was over. I was confident things had gotten better and that my addictions were now a thing of the past. My heart's desire was to help people who had gone through what I believed I had just conquered.

It was a close friend named Dwight who told me I could work as a volunteer with an agency in the city. Their main function was to provide alternative roads for behaviorally-challenged kids and assist with personal matters and housing issues for their families. I thought this would be an excellent opportunity for me: to help someone overcome the pitfalls of life and deposit in their minds the understanding that they were created with destiny.

I was promised that once I served in a capacity of volunteer then the supervisors would see my commitment and hire me as an employee. It wasn't difficult. In fact, I didn't mind doing this for free. I liked what I was doing, and the fact that I was receiving a trade for which most folks spent years in school to receive a degree didn't hurt either.

I had no degree; nonetheless, the agency was so impressed with my performance that they hired me to work full-time as a parent counselor. I believed and desired to take my career much further; therefore, I enrolled in a two-year college, majoring in business administration/computer science. Things couldn't have been more in line, I thought. My newborn son, who was my inspiration and my joy, gave me more incentive to live right. "Finally," I said to myself, "I have something to live for!"

Creating a new life came with learning to handle responsibilities—responsibilities I had long forgotten how to handle. And now I, of all people, was in charge of instructing other folks how to live their lives! Wow! I thought, what a change.

This position allowed me to work with psychiatrists on cases throughout the Cincinnati area. I had access into the Cincinnati Public School System assisting in problem solving. It was through my experiences, good and bad, that they found it useful for me to assist in their methods of transforming an individual's life. I now served as a model for change and facilitated many programs for individuals fighting to conquer the life I had recently escaped.

I was in control of my life again, it appeared, and everything to which I was connected gave me the identity I longed for. "This is the man I was created to be!" I said, in my boisterous pride. "I AM SOMEBODY!" Feeling that as long as I held the briefcase in one hand and the Bible in the other, I was safe.

Unfortunately, the briefcase saw more action than my Bible. I went to church every week, but the part Mom always mentioned— "relationship"—was nowhere to be found.

I did credit all of my accomplishments to Jesus, and knew that if I desired to maintain the life I was now living, then I would have to let go of the friends I once hung around.

I was developing a new name for myself, a far cry from when the negative names presented my identity. Often, after hearing my story, folks would ask if I'd be willing to speak at their youth center or event. That couldn't have served more of an honor for me! "The person who had just been released from prison for defrauding bank machines and passing bad checks!" I thought to myself, "This had to be God!" I was sure of it.

My ego was pumped up beyond measure. All of my success, no matter how real it seemed, was artificial. I think artificial success has a way of making us kind of cocky and forget all about the Blesser. Unknowingly at the time, I found myself compromising everything I had vowed *not* to do.

My vow was to always place God first, then my son, whom I named Jibri. I had even believed the Lord instructed me to change the name of the janitorial company I was trying to establish for the second time. I was certain of being led to take my personal name off of the company and replace it with a more spiritual and God-centered title. I removed the name, "Smith Cleaning Services, Inc." and changed it to "Kingdom Cleaning Services, Inc." No doubt was bucked up against my decision. I was extremely confident that it was the Lord who gave me that command. "But was I truly ready for all this success?" I asked myself. Had I discovered the missing piece to my life? Much was still unanswered. And outside of my job, having my name on a piece of paper stating that I was the owner of a company and the wearing of a shirt and necktie, my life still really had no meaning. Just like days of old, when the OGs confirmed that I was in good standing with the community simply because of my external, the man beneath the clothing was the farthest from my knowing.

The street life wasn't completely out of me, I felt in my soul. No matter how I portrayed that to be false, the strong tug that whispered I was missing something out there emerged with greater force. Sometimes we move way too fast. This I heard from a pastor's message. Nevertheless, I strived fervently to regain if but a fraction of what I had lost in New York and DC I didn't question whether or not I was walking in my ministry; no, my only question was wondering if it was indeed truly my time?

God, who sees all and knows all, knew that I needed much work in my life. He knew I couldn't have the promise until the negative factors in my life were completely erased. Pride was escalating, working its way slowly within almost without notice, it seemed. My attitude towards Denise had fallen into a negative standing. I felt she had mistreated me while I was behind bars so, unconsciously, I held onto the anger. I believed she was a good woman and more importantly a good mother, but the romantic qualities and the motherly intimacy I felt I needed weren't there. It wasn't that she didn't possess those qualities, just that I wasn't mature enough to bring them out of her, I concluded.

Soon I began thinking that I needed a different type of woman, one who possessed what I thought I needed. And before you knew it, I was in the arms of another. Lies and deceit, basically derived from my old nature and behavior came to the forefront. Once again, I found myself acting out the very imagination that danced around in my mind. "I have to fulfill the desire," I said to myself. The urge to revisit a familiar territory was pulsating through my veins at rapid pace. "I've been on the straight and narrow long enough," I said. "Surely I can go back to the neighborhood and mingle a bit."

My thoughts to return to the concrete jungle intensified each day. Scenes of having a good time enticed me even more to tap dance with the underground world again.

Since my job as a parent counselor was formed out of city grant money, when there was no more money available to staff someone for that position I was the one released. I had much idle time on my hands now and wasn't sure what I would do as my days passed. I had brought the janitorial company into existence, but there was no generated income as of yet.

The company offered me a position to work in another section of the organization, but because of my inflated pride I declined. I didn't want any part of working with a bunch of bratty kids; I said, "My position is with adults, people to whom I can relate."

I was trying hard to be one thing on one hand but living a life defined by my position or title on the other. I had no real identity, but the rotating visions of who I wanted to be always stayed clear in my head. I saw myself as a leader, an owner of a company—and not just any company, a major company. The only thing stopping me was the knowledge Dad left for me to discover for myself and a heavy addiction that often found me craving the streets.

The familiar desire to help hurting kids was still buried beneath the superficial image, but my pride stood in the way of allowing me to accept anything I thought was a meaningless title. My goal was to establish a new life for me and my newborn son. I hated the way I had been raised by my parents; and all of my siblings—well, most of my siblings, especially Gail—I detested.

I made my decision to leave the counseling career. What a foolish mistake it was. There was also a high price to pay for doing so, I'll admit. But I was fed up, and thought it was time to move on. The idea that I wouldn't succeed wasn't a consideration. For me, **FAILURE WAS NOT AN OPTION!**

The college I was attending was also becoming a burden. I was making excellent grades, holding a GPA of 3.7 or better; however, my ability to stick to anything for a long period of time had reached its limitation. I was accustomed to throwing in the towel, so to speak. Once things shifted in a direction other than what I had prepared myself for, I'd quit. My "m.o." was quitting, not because I wanted to, I suppose, but because no one ever held me accountable to finish what I started.

School and work were difficult challenges for me, especially since I had just recently been released from prison. I felt I was beginning to suffocate. My plate was too full, and the newest responsibility, my son Jibri, was more than I could handle. I needed a release valve to cleanse me of the things I held inside. It didn't help matters that I was trying to manage two women, along with playing as if I was some sort of loyal churchgoer. I was completely exasperated, and "going back to the old neighborhood couldn't hurt." I reasoned. That's where I knew the parties were going to be happening. "As long as I don't drink, I wouldn't be enticed to do any drugs; after all, drinking was what ignited my craving for cocaine," I told myself. My irrational thinking was full blown. They say in Narcotics Anonymous that relapse starts in the mind, the thought process, then action.

The first time returning to the neighborhood I felt a little as if I had lost a few of my ghetto privileges. I had been absent for some time out there and when that happens, people forget you exist. I had turned semi-nerdish, let them tell it. But it was a foolish mistake on their part to believe anything other than that I was still true to my roots. I didn't care much for the environment of derelicts, nor for the buildings that were dilapidated and unoccupied, but the activities that went on around the community were something I didn't care to relinquish.

"I'm sure I have the addiction kicked; besides, I'm just going there to kill some time," I said, proud that I hadn't used in eleven months. I hadn't considered until later that living on my own was depressing me and, truthfully speaking, I was missing Jibri and his older brother Patrick. It showed that I missed them, often I was at their home more than I was my own. I was in a total state of confusion … again.

I knew to watch TBN (Trinity Broadcast Network) when- ever I needed inspiring. This programming became my own televised Bible instructor. One day, while home on my knees praying for direction, I overheard something on the station that caught my attention. It was people sharing their testimonies of how Jesus had delivered them from all sorts of tribulations and challenges, some of which, I must admit, I didn't believe. Yet something moved me. I had no certainty as to why I had even tuned in to the network that day; I guess I needed some relief, and despite all my many failures and setbacks, the Bible was one place I always found what I was looking for, if only for a moment.

"I'm in my own war!" I said under my breath, as I listened to a few folks who claimed they had been completely delivered from the same addictions. I needed relief and stability in my life. I also needed to know what could grant me total serenity. Mom said, "Jesus!" But according to my understanding, I had Jesus.

I went back to cruise through the neighborhood. The idle mind and desire to engage one more time in what I thought I was missing led me straight to the neighborhood drive-thru to purchase a small Heineken beer. "One won't hurt!" I said, my famous relapse saying. "After this one, I'll go home with some female and that'll be it." Unfortunately, one did hurt. One turned into two. Two turned into three. Three turned into an uncountable amount, and before I knew it, I had rented out my vehicle for dope again, just as I did in the past.

Weeks went by before I regained my vehicle. All of my paycheck had been spent on alcohol, prostitutes, and crack way before I ever saw my vehicle. I walked the neighborhood embarrassed and ashamed of what I had allowed to occur again. My pride was in the dirt now, and all I could see in front of me was red. I was determined to retrieve my vehicle, at all costs. I searched everywhere to find the little dope boys to whom I foolishly rented out my car for a miniature piece of crack rock. I was furious, but mainly at myself. I had allowed "the devil," I called it, to deceive me again. "What's wrong with me?" I asked, reaching a level of boiling. I knew that somebody would pay for my mistake, and thought, "I have to take my frustrations out on someone! Woe to the first person in the line of fire!" I said, vowing to not go home empty-handed. My weeks of neglect regarding my apartment caused me to receive an eviction notice. The letter stated that all of my belongings would be set outdoors if I didn't reply to claim my possessions by a certain date. "How could I reply?" I thought, "I was out chasing crack and my car." I managed to retrieve some of my belongings. But what I wanted most was to handle the kids who kept my car past their deadline! This was war.

Days turned into weeks, and before you knew it, I was homeless, again. This was the sixth time I had tried to abstain, but never found the ability to stay clean. Always there was some reason or another that led to my relapses: pride, cravings, or simply lack of knowledge. I found myself back where I started. I wore the same clothing for days, often bathing at Lannie's house, and believe it or not, my brother Little Man's. Neither of them liked seeing me this way, and even if each of them did carry their own demons, they loved me, I knew, even Gail.

I sat at the bus stop on Madison Road and reflected on when I was a parent counselor, assisting others with their issues. Now here was I, needing someone to assist me.

I thought of the continued trips to the precincts in every community. I was going to jail for minor crimes. Yet it never failed: while I was incarcerated, God would perform His best work. Honestly, I learned more about Jesus during my moments of incarceration than I did in church.

I detested being locked up like some sort of animal. But I came to realize that God spoke to me best when I was forced to be still. Revelation came to me after an episode with Hamilton, Ohio's police department. I was handcuffed, beaten, and sprayed in the eyes and mouth with mace. I had stated far too many times already that it had to stop, but this had to be it. Jibri was turning two years old now, and something had to give, I thought, to myself. He was my primary obligation. There were many other things in life of importance to me, but this was my blood; I had produced him. Besides, I refused to be like so many of the OGs who I knew flat-out neglected their fatherly responsibilities. He was my inspiration. Denise knew that I was a loving father.

She also knew that once I got my life together, I would be a great asset in his life. I loved her for her belief in me, for seeing something in me that at times I couldn't see in myself.

I fought the addiction with everything I had in me; still, I couldn't gain control over the urge that sent me off recklessly, worse than ever. By now, I was completely broke—broke and homeless, again. Even Mom had reached her limit on this one. She no longer allowed me into their home, not because she thought I would steal, but because she believed she had become an enabler to my addiction and that the only way I would ever stop was if she turned her back on me.

One day I stood at the pay phone located at the corner of Madison Road and Whetsel in my neighborhood, the rain thundering down upon me. I had been out in the streets for some days. All of my money was gone, and since the dope was wearing off, I gained an appetite. I thought it would be a good idea to call home, knowing for sure that Mom would give me something to eat.

"Hello, Mom, this is De'Ron. Can I come by and get something to eat, possibly a sandwich or something? I've been out for days."

"I love you, son, but I have to let you go!" she said, vowing that she would no longer contribute to my addiction.

After that, the phone gave signal that there was no one on the other end. The dial tone was a clear indication that she had this time meant what she said. I lingered in the rain awhile in disbelief, stunned at what I just heard and wondering if she had truly meant what she spoke. "I'm her baby," I said, in a saddened slumber. "How could she do this to me?" I asked, "Somebody has to pay!" My first reaction was to make somebody pay.

I walked at a slow pace back in the direction where I knew every crack smoker would be, still unable to shake why Mom had made her statement so adamantly. I didn't belong in the street life anymore, I knew very well. And if I didn't do something to figure out why I kept relapsing, all of what I witnessed around me would be my final state. Becoming like the failed OGs was a nightmare I couldn't live out. I hated the fact that some had allowed life to defeat them. Alleyways served as a safe haven for many. The new morning beckoned them to start their new day with a fresh bottle of whiskey and cigarette. "This can't be the life for me," I said, looking at my surroundings. I was appalled, and I had walked the streets for the last time, I told myself. The instant I snapped out of my shock, I ran back to the telephone I had previously used to call Mom, hoping she'd answer again. I was ready—ready to go to whatever lengths I must in order to discover why I was unable to remain clean. I had no problem with getting clean, but staying clean was another story.

Apparently, I had missed her. That meant I was stuck in the streets to fend for myself for another day. She didn't know that I was ready to go to a drug treatment center. For too long had I tried to do it my way. I knew I needed help. At first, I contested any mentioning of my entering a treatment center. Even Gail, who also had a history along the same lines, suggested that I try a program with sponsors and others who had traveled the identical journey and who were equipped to assist in my recovery.

That was a definite "NO" at the time. But now, as the night approached, my eyelids grew heavy and the blisters on my feet from days of walking told me I had been out there way too long, I was ready to try anything. Thus far, church had been my only remedy, and unfortunately, I hadn't done the job.

Church was a good antidote, I believed; however, the church folks I encountered had absolutely no concept of the type of addiction in which I was trapped. Most of them smirked and gossiped. I even heard rumors that I was a "thug" trying to come into the church to have sex with the girls. Sure, I'll admit that in the early stages of life that had been my agenda, but as I matured a bit, my number one priority was to quit using drugs. I wanted that much more than I wanted any female. The men didn't even try to mentor me. Nevertheless, they never stopped bragging on how their sons were doing in college. That made me a little jealous, I admit. Since all my dad had ever uttered to me were commands, "who wouldn't have some envy?" I concluded at the time. In the meantime, I was rationalizing my disdain for church folks.

It was late, and I guess Mom hadn't answered her phone because she assumed I wanted to beg for money or more food. "I'm forced to journey the night," I told myself quietly. "What am I going to do?" I asked. I had no more money and truthfully no energy to go rob anyone. I wanted a complete change in my life this time, and I believed the place called the CAT HOUSE, a drug treatment facility, could provide what I was looking for. "However, it would have to wait until Mom decides she wants to answer her telephone," I said. I wanted her to take me. "For now, I'm gonna continue gettin' as high as I can!" I headed for the part of town I knew offered me the greatest possibility to get a hit of crack—downtown. Lincoln Courts and Laurel-Homes were two places I was certain to find some old friends who would allow me to join in. I had no money, so if I was to receive any type of high it would have to be a free one. I was tired of searching and my broken, exhausted body needed to collapse somewhere. Washington Park, a place where the bums hung out, was the closest place I could find a moment's rest. I really had no desire to sit in a place that I perceived to be "skid row." But it was nighttime now, and I was growing sleepy.

I managed to hustle-up enough change to buy me a beer. I figured I would sit on the bench a while and quench my thirst. Everyone knew that this was a man's last stop. Anyone who ended up in this atmosphere was either already defeated or on their way to defeat. Nothing worth hanging around for was found in this area. In fact, this is the place where those in church who wanted to give themselves a pat on the back and go home feeling as if they had done God a service and their eternal reward was secure, who would come to pass out sodas and sandwiches or whatever pamphlets from church they had. Then when that period of sharing God's good grace was ended, the derelicts were left to fend for themselves.

I located an empty bench away from everyone. I was still wearing the clothes that were in good condition; even my shoes, believe it or not, still had a shine to them—if I wiped them with a dry cloth. It was obvious I didn't belong there, at least in my eyes. My mind and my emotions fought to make sense of how I now sat in a place of despair. There was no making sense of it. It made no sense. No matter how I tried to justify it or rationalize my actions, I was to blame for the place I now sat.

ALL HOPE IS GONE

I sat on the park bench with tears in my eyes focusing intently at the forty-ounce bottle of Old English 800 still in its brown paper bag. I didn't care who saw me. I scanned the area carefully. Down the street, about a quarter mile, I noticed there was a light on at one of the homeless shelters. "What am I thinking?" quickly shaking myself from the crazy notion that I could ever stay at one of those places.

Then, returning to my self-discussion, I asked myself, "But where am I going to sleep?" I was completely worn out, and even a hit of crack wouldn't be enough for me to begin another phase of disastrous living. Nah, I decided, it was time to throw in the towel and start my life off fresh. I had no choice; the homeless shelter it was.

I looked at the bottle of beer in my right hand angrily, as if it had just kicked me in the stomach. The word "poison" made its way from my mouth. I found myself repeating it. "Poison," I said and, before slamming the entire bottle to the ground, addictively took one last sip. I resented the choice I was about to make, but resented Denise and my mother even more for not allowing me to stay with either of them. I dragged myself from the park bench and began walking towards the dreadful building, still in awe as to how I ended up at a homeless shelter when I was doing so well. I continued placing one foot in front of the other, knowing that if I stopped at any time I would turn in the opposite direction. When I finally approached the shelter, I noticed they were holding a church session. The music was lively, I thought; actually, I liked what I was hearing.

I entered the sanctuary slowly, as if afraid or indecisive. Finding my way midway to the front, desperate to hear something to reassure me, I sat down next to a poor, dusty gentleman who smelled as if he hadn't bathed in weeks. He really made me look closely at my life. In fact, everyone in the sanctuary brought a different glimpse of what my future entailed. I was speechless.

At the end of the service an announcement was made over the speaker instructing everyone who wished to stay to proceed downstairs to receive the evening meal. It was further mentioned, "All doors will be looked and no one will be permitted to leave the building until the 6:00 a.m. wake-up!" I followed the instructions to relocate downstairs to the place where the evening meal would be served. However, while I was marching with the other men, I couldn't help but notice the enthusiasm Ibeheld from their facial expressions. I saw in them the commitment of contentment as they received their meal that disgusted my appetite. I was extremely hungry, but not enough to eat something I had trouble describing. Yet still I extended both hands to retrieve the tray of soup (or something that resembled soup), grabbed a seat at the long table, and sat down as comfortably as I could force myself to be.

I took a serious gaze at my surroundings for the second time, trying to decide if this is where I really wanted to be. In an instant, my eyes began to water. "This is truly a sad sight to see." I said to myself. "How could men have succumbed to this? Is this really happening to me, as well?" I couldn't withstand viewing anymore of the trepidation. "This isn't me; I'm better than this!" I exclaimed.

"I have to leave this place!" I tried to convince myself that the decision I was about to make was the right one. I knew the alarm would go off. They made a special commitment to let everyone know that this place was highly protected. I didn't care. "I'm not about to sleep here." I said, that I was sure of.

I pushed my tray of soup over to the gentleman sitting to my right; it was received with gratitude, it seemed. Without hesitation, I walked towards the exit sign that pointed in the direction I was looking for. I leaped up the stairs, a few of them at a time to speed up the process of getting out of the dismal atmosphere. Fnally reaching the door that separated me from the outside world, I thrust the door open and quickly took off running down the street as fast as I could. I was sure the abrupt sound startled everyone. Many of the men probably wondered who and why someone would want to leave a warm place to sleep, not to mention a hot meal. (I'm not degrading any of the men who live life according to their misfortune … gosh, no! The only thing I would like to point out is the fact that, we *all* have **choices**. Our choices have positive or negative consequences. And at that point, I had made the decision to choose another direction.) As I ran down the dark street, bypassing the park from which I had first made my decision, I glanced back to see if there was anyone following me for whatever reason. I didn't think I had violated any law; nonetheless, I secured my assumption. Once I was clear out of sight, I found a spot where I believed I could rest long enough to catch my breath, and to figure out what I would do for the remainder of the night. There were no places for me to go. All of my family disowned me due to the lying, stealing, and cheating I had done. Once again, I sat motionless at my crossroad before reaching the conclusion to walk in town, hoping to see someone from whom I could possibly receive a small pittance.

Downtown was vacant. It appeared the only person out in the night hour was me. My thoughts unrhythmically danced around in my head, just as always. What I contemplated was beyond my capability. I was a nomad, wandering aimlessly in the city streets of Cincinnati, just as I had out East.

I could walk no further. My legs and feet had indicated to me that they had taken enough abuse. Early morning was slowly creeping upon me, and there were no more trips around the block I could make. I needed to find somewhere cozy to lay my head … just for a little while, I thought.

The nearest hotel looked as if it would suffice. I withdrew inside as if I was interested in purchasing a room and noticed someone I knew. I explained to him my situation and in sympathy, I'm sure, he told me where I could hide out until the morning.

The place suggested was inside a vacant corner that contained a few seats and sofas. He said that security never paid any attention to guests who slept in those chairs, and that for the night, I'd be fine!

I wasn't sure how long I had been asleep; all I knew was that a hand was on my shoulder, rocking me. Then, as my eyes opened, and my focus came into play, I realized it was a security guard. His first words were, "Do you have a room in this hotel, sir?"

"No" I responded. "Well then, sir, you must leave the hotel, immediately."

I was too worn out to put up a fuss; besides, I was in the wrong, so, I did as instructed. I did manage to sleep until the sun came up, however. But now I was still faced with the same problem I had the night before: no money and no place to reside permanently.

It had been a long night, not to mention a few long weeks. This was another awful relapse. All I did was stay in the streets getting high and roamed from house to house to bathe. I came to the conclusion that I couldn't repeat another binge like the one I just endured. "Whatever I must do, whatever it takes, I'll do it!" I said to myself.

My only decision left was to call Mom and ask for one more chance to prove that I was truly ready to change my life. I pan-handled the change from a stranger to make the call. The introduction was always the same.

"Hello, Mom, it's me," I said. As we proceeded through our exchange, she made a suggestion I had never considered. "Why don't you ask Valerie if you can stay with her? That is, if you are truly ready to change your life."

"What choice do I have?" I thought. I didn't know her that well, but I had no choice. Another round similar to the one I had just endured —I couldn't foresee it.

"Okay, you check with her, then let me know, okay? But in the meantime, Mom, would you mind if I came by the house to bathe and grab a bite to eat? I'm really ready this time," I concluded.

"Sure, come on by." she replied.

When I arrived at their home, the familiar look protruded from her face. Dad again had nothing much to say. And if he did say something, it generally wasn't anything I cared to hear. Mom and I spoke for a while before I asked if she had spoken to Valerie. She mentioned she had, and that Valerie asked if she could pray on the decision.

I felt I let Mom down again. The battle I was fighting in order to make her proud—well, I guess I was losing, I considered. She wanted the best for me, I knew—in fact, for all of us. And even if she did make her mistakes in life, she was a good mother and I wanted to take away her belief that she had failed. I wasn't making a good impression of someone who would become someone significant in life, I knew. However, at any and all cost, I vowed that I would ultimately succeed!

The word I was waiting to hear came as a relief! Valerie cared deeply about my mother and knew very well that I was my mother's baby boy whom she loved deeply. In part, I believe that's why she allowed me to stay at her home in the beginning. But also, Valerie shared with me that she believed I was genuinely a good person with an outstanding determination to succeed outside of the drugs and alcohol. I knew she was a bit apprehensive about the arrangement; she was going through transitions of her own and really needed the space and alone time for herself. Nevertheless, despite her feelings, she stepped out on *faith*.

"I won't take long before I get back on my feet," I assured her. She had witnessed my drive and determination before and believed that I could make it. I had commitment to pursue my dream, but what I was lacking, and in drastic need of was, some **staying power!**

Jibri needed me, and I was determined that nothing was going to interfere with my being an active dad in his life! He was still an infant; therefore, "I have time to get my life in balance," I told myself. This was my goodbye to Denise. I knew I had to move on, just as she had with her life. If I were to become anything in life, I first needed to discover what my triggers were.

Valerie's house consisted of nothing but Christian music and Christian video tapes of T.D. Jakes, Joyce Myers, Rod Parsley and many other highly recognized preachers. The environment was definitely something I needed. The serenity it gave allowed me to recuperate in peace. And she never put any pressure on me.

Just as Mom had done, she allowed me to rest for a couple of weeks until I was at the point where I could go out and submit a few resumes. "I'm so tired of starting over, always the same procedure. I really don't have any more energy to start over again. This has to be the final episode!" I told myself.

Finding employment was never a problem. I was fairly skilled at charming the interviewer and was quick on my feet. If someone gave me the chance to come in for an interview, it was ninety-nine percent in my favor. My first job, returning to the workforce after my binge was with a gas station and food store as an assistant manager. I applied for the position and was called back for the first interview in a matter of two weeks.

The complete process to hire me consisted of two interviews. Soon, after the second go-around, I was hired on the spot. Nevertheless, my employment was short lived due to the fact that I had lied on my application by answering *no* to the question asking if I had ever been convicted of a felony. I thought that they wouldn't actually check.

My life on a rollercoaster ride continued. There were still a few triggers I was unaware of that caused me to fall two more times. These relapses were small in comparison to the others. Each of these lasted no more than at most two days. I paid a high price to learn about the disease and its triggers that caused me to want to commit suicide, hurt other people, rob and steal, and do unthinkable things. I was growing fully convinced that if I was to ever become victorious, total surrender to God and learning for myself about the God of whom Mom spoke so passionately would be my only hope!

My transformation wouldn't dare come without a "hell" of a fight. I was bound by ignorance, and the Christian life I tried relentlessly to develop remained hindered by what is plainly referred to in the Bible as

SIN. I no longer engaged in alcohol or drugs, but sin and its pleasures were equally addictive. Follow me and let me explain!

A HARD FIGHT

THE price had to be paid, and surely nothing I had acquired came easy. My biggest war was with my spirit man, the battle urging me to do wrong when I really wanted to do right. "If only I could control that …" I'd often tell myself. I was attending church regularly again. This time, I guess since I was now several years older and much wiser, going exclusively for the females wasn't my priority. My heart and desire to get to know Jesus was sincere.

I admit that, until then I didn't understand that there were two Gods and one Jesus offering prosperity, peace, joy, eternal life, and blessings overflowing unto three and four generations to come: There was the other god, Satan, who offered me nothing but momentary pleasure and eternal damnation. The other god sucked life completely out of me, dissipating my spirit as if concealed in an excessively dark cave where the only existence of life would be the shadow of a projected face that managed to somehow escape from the nemesis of its surroundings. This would be my fight to forcefully grab hold to the diminishing light that was my only hope of escape.

Things in the world of business brought about unconceivable joy! Actually, walking in the reality of what I had envisioned assured me all the more now that this was surely my divine destiny. Hiring folks to work for my company gave me such a rush. I was determined to give God the full praise.

Being referred to as president or CEO (chief executive officer) was to me a sign that I was chosen to accomplish something great! Thinking this to myself, my ego inflated from every thought of the fact that I was in charge. "I should have been dead," I said, holding a quiet conversation within.

I was at peace with the way my business venture was headed. Eight months into it and already I had landed contracts with some of the major companies. I even became a member of one of Cincinnati's business organizations. "I'm on a roll!" I said, rendering a pat on the back for successfully coming to the life I had now obtained. I was proud of my accomplishment, and so was Mom!

The number seven biblical doctrine was finally beginning to pay off, I thought, and said in assurance that "I'm *never* going to look back. I made it!"

Business progressed rapidly, and my worship service on Sundays served as my way of saying thanks to God for bringing me so far. Yet, there was still something missing, I believed. I saw other men in business that drove the fanciest cars, and I knew had pockets full of money. I didn't have a fancy car, but I wanted one. And, even though business was flourishing, I didn't possess a pocket full of money, no matter how badly I wanted it. I did not want to be outdone. "My reputation is on the line," I said. "Who can compete with me in business?" That other enemy called *pride* was getting the best of me. "I,I,I," was all I could see; I gave no glory to God. It was all about me.

Despite the good progress of the business, I wanted more, and I wanted it to come much faster than it was coming. Greed and impatience ran throughout my inner parts. I couldn't wait for it, as Mom had suggested. I wanted it now! I played the role of a big shot, so now it was time for me to look the part as well, I thought. There was no way I could allow myself to look upon so many other folks with their material possessions and not produce my own. My mental condition was becoming tainted with desire for wealth and my spiritual condition was declining from the lack of spiritual food (God's Word); "You are what you eat," I'd always say.

The desire to be "The Man" was my lust and now my first priority. I wanted the best cleaning equipment, the most employees, and the best company vehicles. After conniving, I discovered a way I could save lots of money: "I'll hire some of the neighborhood crack smokers!" I said to myself. My second thought was that I could earn a little extra cash on the side to bring my desire into fruition. "The little extra cash would be a big help," I told myself. I had no time to waste, I thought. The million dollars I wanted was staring me right in the face and I looked for a way to justify this foul, deceptive thinking. I rationalized that the more vehicles I had, the more work I could ultimately take on, and the more work I took on, the more employment I could provide to the city. What thinking? All of the rationalization led me right back to my number one ambition: to make money.

I ached inside from the pain of wanting to gain wealth, so much so that one day when I could fight the temptation no longer, I approached a friend in lieu of a proposition. His life and occupation consisted of being a full-time drug dealer. I knew if anybody was able to get me started, he'd be the one. I had dealt with him in the past, but mainly only as a "gofer" to pick-up packages that came into the city. I was a user of the drug back then, but now this was different. I wanted to join the ranks of the dealers. I knew there was no more desire to use any type of drug, nor to drink alcohol. I stood in great confidence of that and told myself that if I was given a chance, I could be the biggest drug dealer in the city … if I chose! But my goal wasn't to be a big-time dealer initially; all I wanted was to earn enough cash to purchase the things I needed.

The guy I chose to connect with was heavily involved in running a million-dollar operation. His connections were huge and stretched throughout many other cities and states. Since we were like family, I knew he'd accept my request. Besides, he mentioned how proud he was of my life's turnaround and that he would do anything for me. He said, "Just call me." For a moment I wrestled with his proposal. I knew it was something I wanted to do, but on the other hand, there was a little fear. "Did I really care to get that deeply involved?" I asked myself. But as the hunger for material possessions and image increased, I considered this would be the only way I would ever obtain it. I gave it all the consideration I was going to give it and told myself, "This is going to happen!" Finally hearing from me, he asked, "How much do you want to distribute?"

"As much as possible," I replied. I had new ideas on how I would construct my million-dollar empire. No matter how it came about, I was determined to build the company I dreamed of building, at all costs. I was determined to achieve my goal! My plan was to pay the crack smokers in cash and crack, the majority of their earnings coming via the crack. I knew I was unable to pay them completely in crack because of tax purposes. I had to report some earned wages to the payroll company

I had obtained to make the business more legit. I had to do this as proof to the IRS that I was withdrawing taxes from my employees; my master plan was going well for the first year, I cared to believe. Mom could no-longer withstand watching me sell my soul to the devil, I guess. She noticed the rapid growth of material possessions I had acquired, but respectfully gave me her motherly advice. She emphasized the fact of how "you need faith," and how "you should learn to wait on Jesus." I really wasn't trying to hear that, not at the moment, I said to myself. She stressed how the Lord had brought me from such a long way and how He was blessing me with more than I ever had in my life. She was correct, but I assured her that I did have faith and that my involvement would only be temporary. I assured her that the street life was out of my system ... at least the part of hanging out, going to parties, drinking, and looking for females.

I learned a lot from my past occurrences, so much so that life itself was no longer oppressing to me. I was completely devoid of what used to appear as fun. Now my main goal was to make a better life for my son Jibri.

My Sunday morning church ritual was reaching a major decline. I no longer possessed the energetic fervor that once accelerated my praise and worship! In fact, I felt like the biggest hypocrite for coming into the house of God, and then within seconds would be distributing mass quantities of cocaine throughout the city.

I hated the party scenes and the lifestyle of drinking and getting high. I wanted no part ... ever again! I stayed mostly indoors. Whenever I wasn't out making a delivery, anyone could find me sitting on the sofa in my home. I did absolutely nothing outside of making money and occasionally reading my Bible that lay opened on my coffee table. I enjoyed reading my Bible, even if I still didn't fully understand much of the language. I watched the smokers run throughout the night hours, just as I had done in the past. This was my second year as a dealer. I was on the other side of the game now, and life still didn't appear as full as I thought it would be when I had all I strived for at the tip of my fingers.

My conscience began to annoy me. I started receiving guilty feelings for selling the drugs that once upon a time had me tangled and in bondage. Often, I'd pause to stare at someone whom one of my workers would serve (a street phrase meaning *to distribute*). I didn't like what I was witnessing, especially a pregnant woman coming to try and receive her daily fix. Mom had raised me better than that, at least.

The atmosphere was chaotic. People were running from here to there looking for their next hit and fighting because one person said that the other stole their cocaine. Cars were in and out of the area day and night in search of their fix. It never ended, and I was growing sick and tired of contributing to such madness.

I prayed for God to release me from my newest addiction of selling cocaine or even the money and power that came along with it. I was ready to serve God, I told myself, but knew I couldn't fully serve Him with all of the baggage I still carried. My mind never rested. And at night, at all hours, I found myself sleeping with one eye open and my hand underneath my pillow with my finger gripping a .380 caliber handgun for protection. This lifestyle was becoming a big headache. I no-longer enjoyed building my house based upon the blood, sweat, and tears of folks who eventually lost their homes and some even their families. I could no longer sit back and watch that take place, I said to myself, fighting the tears from the emotional touch of God's presence, I suppose. I knew that I was going through another change. Even the money brought no real joy. Sure, it helped in financing material items. The money, street credibility, and artificial power blinded me.

The drug addicts out in the streets reminded me of myself; the visual would confirm.

I hurt deeply inside, and asked God if He could ever forgive me. Torment was taking place, even inside of my home, which no one knew. In the midnights, I would awaken only to find lying next to me a puddle of sweat and tears. Immediately I slid off of my bed and fell to my knees, looking for relief from the horrific nightmare encountered. In this dream there were people who had overdosed returning from the grave—I couldn't sleep.

Repeatedly, I told God how sorry I was for breaking my vow to Him when I was in prison. I honestly had the nerve to ask God if He would bless my evil deeds, that if He would just allow me to make enough money to buy more vans, then I would stop. What nerve!

No one knew of my discontent to sell drugs anymore except my right-hand man, Gerald. He was closer to me than anyone. Often, I would mention to him how tired I was of seeing people strung out on crack. "How could I?" I always thought to myself, reflecting back to when four of us in my family were hooked on the drug. I knew the damage crack would cause in a person's life, but in the beginning it didn't matter; all I could see was money!

The dreams intensified, almost unbearably. I didn't take heed of the warnings telling me to stop selling, nor to the scripture I'd always manage to turn to. Regardless of where I turned in the Bible, it always seemed to go right back to the same scripture.

In one service at church, I tried hard to maintain a spirit of praise and to worship. I tried desperately to give a shout, but my feelings of hypocritical behavior wouldn't allow my mouth to utter a word. My spirit had been wounded and sin had become too great for me to conquer on my own. I stood up in the middle of the service as one in pursuit of the restroom. In actuality, I was checking to see what would be the shortest route to make my exit. The church environment was too much for me to bear. I had become completely engulfed in the lifestyle. And no matter how much I abhorred what I was doing, breaking free wasn't coming easy.

Outside in my car there were ten ounces of crack cocaine stashed in the glove compartment ready for distribution to anxious customers in other neighborhoods. "How could I?" This was my famous question to myself whenever reality set in as to what I was doing to God's people. The shame I had inside should have been more than enough to stop me from doing wrong. But despite my excessive hatred for the negative lifestyle, the love for money and material possessions kept me connected. The sad truth is I believed I could stop selling at any time. That's what I told myself. I even told Mom that whenever I wanted to stop, I could.

I was slipping away, deeper than I knew. Many days of fighting with my spirit was beginning to take effect. Inside my spirit, I concluded that I'd rather have Jesus than all the money in the world; but on the outside, my life completely represented everything except Jesus. I knew God was the only person able to completely deliver me. I knew of God, and believed in all the power He possessed, but I didn't have patience nor faith, as Mom would say. The kind of faith I perceived was needed in order to truly testify the way I saw ministers like Rod Parsley, Joyce Myers, T.D. Jakes, and countless others. I could *never* make the sort of proclamation any of those preachers made, I knew, without total faith. I believed in God, Jesus as the Son of God … the whole nine yards; however, I had a problem giving "everything" to either of them. That was my problem.

I completely contaminated my business, the business I believed God had given me. The primary intent was to help individuals in need and provide employment. Well, I provided employment, all right.

Out of nowhere, many unfortunate circumstances began happening, things I couldn't explain. All I know is that it had to be designed. It wasn't uncommon for me or anyone in that particular lifestyle to carry a pistol; everyone pretended to be Al Pacino from the movie *Scarface*. I had developed a more quiet, reserved attitude, but I wasn't weak. I was now a supplier to many of the guys who once sold me drugs. That, to me, was the highlight of the lifestyle.

Constantly, I fought the spirit of good versus evil I harbored inside, not knowing how to maintain the Christian life I viewed many others carrying out. I wanted a normal life, a life free from so much worry and stress. It was the misery inside that produced the anger; I had no problem understanding that. I was an angry child, so naturally I became an angry adult. My workers also knew that I could be dangerous. A few of them had to learn the hard way. One in particular thought he'd try me, I guess, probably not believing I would do anything. He was wrong. After realizing that I was short $1,500.00, I called him in, allowing him an opportunity to rectify the situation. Apparently, he wanted to stick to his story that everything I had given him to sell was accounted for. I had heard all I wanted to hear anymore. I pulled the .380 caliber from out of my pants, and before I knew, blood was coming from his mouth. "Open ya mouth!" I told him. Although hesitant, he obeyed, and the .380 caliber was sliding inward, resting upon his tongue.

My most precious pastime was roller skating. Every Thursday at the Fun Factory is where I found solitude. I was able to escape for a while the madness of the drug dealer's life style and be a normal citizen, just for one night! However, on this particular night, an ex-female-friend and I got into a little altercation. Exchanging words that reinforced their meaning from the attached facial expression, things became heated inside of the skating rink. This was the only night for gospel skate. I chose this day for skating because it was the calmest. And, some part of me wanted to stay connected to the church scene.

During our verbal exchange, I suppose I said something that didn't sit well with her. She had spread a rumor that I was still using crack cocaine. I confronted her statement. The guy she told that to had worked for me for quite a while and knew it wasn't true.

I wanted to punch her right in her mouth, gave it serious consideration, then thought against it for fear of everyone witnessing. She wanted someone to notice that we were having this argument. I say that because her voice level grew higher and higher.

Apparently, she was entertaining the same thought I had regarding hitting her. It wasn't seconds after my consideration that, out of nowhere—BAM! She slapped me with everything she had! Immediately I ran to take off my skates. I knew I couldn't let this go down, I thought, while in route . I was furious! I knew it would be best if I left the rink, but as I made my way to the exit door, she commented, "De'Ron, I ain't scared of you." And as if she was some sort of idiot, she took off her skates and followed me outside. That was a very bad decision on her part. Without hesitation, I returned the slap. WHAP! I noticed her entire body crashing against the wall. Apparently, she didn't believe I would hit her. It wasn't something I participated in on a regular basis. I had outgrown hitting woman, for the most part, but this was an exception to the rule. In disbelief, she trotted towards her car. When I noticed the trunk of her car upward, my first instinct was that she was retrieving a pistol. Violence could come from anyone, was my first thought. I had to be on guard at all times. I wasted no time in unlocking my car door to reach in my glove compartment to retrieve the smaller of my two guns, a .25 caliber. The other was my gold baby, my .380 caliber. I knew I couldn't pull out the larger pistol; I would have killed her if she was hit by one of those bullets. My intent was to only scare.

I gave her three warnings to close the trunk of her car. Her resistance made me that much more paranoid. I wasn't sure what she was actually looking for, all I knew was that I wasn't about to "come up short," as we say. My impulse was to fire the first shot immediately. After her refusal to heed my warnings, the next sound she heard was Pow… Pow… Pow! "I told you to get out of your trunk," I said to her. I completely forgot to recover the empty casings that fell to the ground. That was enough evidence for the city police to find something they could charge me with.

It wasn't until two weeks later I had returned to the very skating rink where the incident occurred. How stupid of me, I thought. Before

I could roll around the skating floor three good laps, an announcement came over the loudspeaker stating that I must report to the front door. Deep inside, I felt it had something to do with discharging the firearm. Before I made it to the location, I noticed a gentleman pointing me out to the sheriff waiting near the place I had to report. "Uh, oh," I said to myself. There was no doubt in my mind that the police officer was there to escort me out of the building. "What have I gotten myself into?" this time mumbling underneath my breath and careful not to let him see my nervousness.

When I finally reached the spot where he was standing, abruptly he asked, "Are you Mr. Smith?"

"I am. Why do you ask?" I replied. He really didn't care to answer me inside the skating rink, I guess. Motioning in the direction of the door that led to the hallway, this time his voice exerted more authority to let me know he was the one in control; he began reading me my Miranda rights.

Once out of view of all attendees at the rink, carefully he placed the handcuffs on me and told me that I was going to jail for discharging a firearm. I didn't argue. How could I? After all, he was telling the truth. Fortunately, before I had made my way to the officer, I had given my car keys to a friend.

I was frantic the entire ride to the station. I hoped and prayed they wouldn't discover which car in the parking lot was mine. I wanted my friend to drive it to my house. Even my friend didn't know that there was an ounce of crack in the glove compartment, so there was no way I wanted the officers to discover that. I surely didn't want my friend to get connected, especially when he was just an innocent bystander.

Immediately upon reaching the police station, I requested to call my attorney, a guy I had met while walking through downtown. I was coming from an appointment I had with a possible client of my janitorial company. He and I became pretty good friends. For the most part, I admired his integrity. He came across as super knowledgeable pertaining to the law. I really had no reason to distrust him, so with that he won me over.

I waited almost an hour at the station before they allowed me to make my phone call. It was after 10:00 p.m. by now, and I figured he'd be asleep or not wanting to be disturbed. "This is an emergency; he's about to wake up!" I thought to myself.

I brought him up to date as best I could under the time restraint the officer allowed. I gave him the most important details of the situation. "I'll be there in forty-five minutes; sit tight!" he said in his raspy voice. I could tell I woke him up, but I didn't care; this was an emergency. His statement was comforting to hear, I thought, and was certain that when he arrived I'd be walking out of the precinct doors with him!

When he did finally arrive within the timeframe of his estimation, he bypassed everyone except the officer at the booking desk. I heard him ask for the papers that contained the cause of my arrest. I felt relieved to have him there, knowing that I had enough money to pay his fee, and for that reason alone, he was going to have me released … ASAP!

I noticed a dim look of disappointment on his face.

"What's the problem?" I asked.

"You have to stay the night in the county justice center," he said.

"Go to jail?" I said abruptly. "You must be kiddin' me. I can't go to jail; I have a cleaning company to run!" finalizing my stance on the subject.

"Don't worry, I'll get you off the hook, but there's nothing I can do for you tonight," he concluded.

"I guess I have no choice. For tonight at least, the county jail will be my resting place, huh?" I accepted the fact that I wouldn't be going home to sleep in my king-size bed.

After assuring me that he would definitely be in court in the morning to request a bond, we shook hands. I plopped in the seat located at the in-processing desk, amazed at what was happening to my life. "So many close calls," I pondered.

Then, awakened by the officer telling me to follow him as he led me to the prisoners' holding tank, he stated, "You'll be in there until they're ready to transport you to the county. Sit tight." That seemed to be the famous ending from everyone who didn't have to worry about going home, I said in my haste.

The night in the county provided me with some well needed time to sort things out and reflect on how my life was all of sudden changing, but not for good. All remembrances of my mother's words bombarded me as I fought hard to justify everything I was doing, believing somewhat that it was God who had allowed me to develop my business from crack sales. And since I hadn't been caught when many times I was pulled over—inside my compartment lay at least $10,000 in cash, half of that in drugs— there was no doubt I was in good standing with the man upstairs.

My ritual behind bars was consistent. The first thing I always grabbed was a Bible. Second, the quiet time incarceration provided granted time to reflect on how my life was going. Each time I took advantage of the situation, no matter how unfortunate it seemed. It served as a tool for correction. Of course, I hated the fact of being caged like an animal, but the aftereffects were worth the punishment.

I wanted a miraculous transformation, nonetheless, not understanding that the prayers I prayed to grant me wisdom, understanding, and new character were taking place right under my nose.

I recall praying that I wanted to be made in Jesus's image and used for His kingdom! The process of purging was happening, though through lack of understanding and little faith, I couldn't grasp the fact that conversion meant going through the fire of life before I could come forth as pure gold, as quoted in the Bible. I wanted the gold part, but the fire I could do without, I thought.

I overlooked any warning indicating that I should stop what I was doing. It wasn't until incident number three that a light finally clicked on in my head telling me that God was speaking. This was the last straw. I managed to escape a gun charges and driving with cocaine in my car because the officer hadn't found it. I had several trips to the precinct, suspensions, bullets grazing across my chest and more … but now, I figured, the Lord had had enough; things were about to get really hot!

My attorney had managed to have the charged reduced to inducing panic with a firearm. This carried a maximum of six months in jail and a fine, or, six months' probation with an ankle bracelet. That was nothing, I thought, "I can do that standing on my head," as we say in jail. I didn't really care to do jail time and especially didn't care to have a dog's bracelet around my leg, monitoring me like I was some sort of lab experiment. The trial went back and forth for a month or so. The judge wanted to know if I still had the gun that I used that night. He stated that he wanted a gun off the streets, and that if I turned in the gun, he'd dismiss the assault charge. I didn't believe him; everyone knew that a gun charge was an automatic three-year prison sentence. Despite my apprehension, I gave the missing pistol to my attorney to turn in and trusted in God.

Every court hearing, the girl came only in hopes to see me put away. She had lied and exaggerated some of the circumstances. Her main goal was to do whatever she could to have me serve jail time. But it wasn't in the cards on that occasion because I walked scot-free. When the judge passed down his ruling, the entire courtroom gasped at his decision. Even I was amazed at his ruling. My ego swelled all the more, assured that my money to the attorney was the reason for my release. I discredited the hours of prayers prayed.

I told Mom that I was finished selling any type of narcotics. I promised to her that I would do the right thing in God's sight. Whether she believed me or not, I'm not sure. Nonetheless, I wasn't going to concern myself with her doubt, I had something to prove. I was extremely grateful that I had not gone to prison—that time.

It seemed the moment I made that vow, business began to decline. But as desperately as I wanted to take illegal measures, I remembered my vow to Mom. I was sincere in my promise, but things were heating up to the point that I couldn't bear to sit back and wait for something to happen. I was afraid that all would be lost if I didn't do something quickly. This was my baby and just like any parent, I couldn't sit by and watch my baby die.

I sat on my sofa wrestling with the desire to do wrong, fluttering back and forth with questions running through my mind: why I should versus why I shouldn't. I took one look at the Bible that lay open on my coffee table. I decided to flip through a few pages just to see if any magic would come through to remove the thoughts that I was entertaining. Just as always, the same scripture appeared and read, "Wealth gotten by vanity will be diminished."

I couldn't compete with the probing desire. After weeks of declining business, greed and foolish thinking deluded me once again. I needed repairs for my vehicles badly. The fact that I wanted to "keep up with the Joneses" also pressed me to do the very thing I vowed not to do. The mental manipulation ran deep. I told myself continuously that this time I would sell only to purchase the well-needed repairs, but the momentum took on a life of its own.

The beginning of the end was when I was reintroduced to a former drug dealer who had been out of the swing of things for quite a while. Out of nowhere, he showed up asking if he could get hooked up with some "weight" (a large quantity). His timing was perfect, I thought! I needed the extra cash, and this was just the deal I was looking for! We went on for weeks discussing how he could get what he was looking for. I told him that personally "I don't have that much weight, but I can get it." I wanted this deal to go down, never thinking for once about the fact that he appeared suddenly from nowhere. I didn't do any research, as I was supposed to. I made my first mistake in trusting him—a big no-no.

We met each other regularly, but still hadn't conducted any transactions, just verbal agreements. I agreed to the amount he stated he was looking to spend, assured that I would get my cut of the profit. I mentioned that I would introduce him to my supplier, if he accepted my recommendation.

"Agreed," he said.

My supplier also agreed to the arrangement. I guess it was on my word that he did so. The day of the transaction we arranged to be at my home and office. "My partner'll be handling the deal," I told him.

"That's fine!" he said. "As long as I get what I'm looking for, I don't care who handles it."

"I hear dat," I replied.

"On the other hand," he said, "before I purchase a lot, let me just buy an ounce to see how the dope fiends like it."

"I don't have a problem with that," I said. "I guarantee you … you'll be back!"

A few days later he called me on my car cell phone to tell me that the crack addicts loved it!

"I told you." I said, proud that we had the best dope in the city.

"Do you have anything?" he asked me.

"No, I don't," I replied, "but let me give my partner a call and I'll get back with you."

Later that same day I tried feverishly to reach my partner to arrange the new deal. I knew he loved money just as much as I did, so after many attempts to reach him and he not returning my call, I knew something was wrong. The other guy hadn't returned any of my calls, either. "As bad as he wants our product, now he's not responding. I don't like it," I said to myself.

The whole day was a wreck. An eerie feeling hovered over the atmosphere. Besides, I needed some dope for myself to serve my customers. I mentioned to a waiting buyer that it would be some time before I'd be back in the swing of things. "What's going on?" I said to myself.

Hours later I received a phone call telling me that the two of them had already met. I was unaware that the two of them had exchanged phone numbers during their first encounter. I was ticked off at the fact that they both went behind my back and excluded me. My partner was now his sole supplier, excluding me altogether. I had no more to do with this guy; in fact, I wanted to shoot him for betraying me.

I can't count the number of times they'd met. But the day came when I was unable again to reach my partner. I took it as if he was just out of town this time. I knew he would be making a trip to set up a new deal; therefore, I dismissed the fact that he hadn't answered. It wasn't until the next day that I had made another attempt to reach him. By now, he would have responded to my emergency page, I told myself.

That afternoon, I received a telephone call from another partner in the business, asking me if I had heard what happened to "C."

"No," I responded. He proceeded to tell me that "C" had been arrested, and that the guy to whom I had introduced him was an informant for RENU, an undercover drug enforcement unit.

"What!" I said. I couldn't believe what I was hearing. I sat at the computer in my office area, bewildered and in shock. "I can't believe this," telling myself for the final time. "What in God's name have I done?" I said, slamming my fist on the desk.

I justified the occurrence by saying that it was his fault. "If he hadn't tried to be greedy, I would be in that situation," I said, looking for some comfort to appease the mess I had made.

"Has a bond been set yet?" I asked him.

"No," he replied, "He won't receive one until his arraignment in the morning."

"Cool," I said. "I'll be in the courtroom tomorrow and will give you a call afterwards."

"Bet," he replied, hanging up the phone on that note.

My whole world was beginning to crumble. Despite the fact that I no longer used any form of narcotics nor indulged in alcohol, I realized that the only time my life had any real significance is when I was fully committed to serving Jesus. That truth I couldn't reject. I wondered if what it said in Jeremiah, Chapter 1, Verse 5 was actually true: "I knew you before you were formed in your mother's womb …" I desired to believe everything I read in the Bible but just as it was when I was a child, some things seemed too farfetched—which hindered me from total surrender.

Mom said that I must "let go and let God." I was afraid, no doubt, and wondered what would occur if I truly did let go? My mind swarmed in total disarray. I was in this great big world looking for answers. My childhood circulated continuously with horrific memories of my past, and I had no one to lend a helping hand in my rescue. My decisions and my choices were my own, my life and my destiny. "If I wanted to lend any portion of it to God, that was my decision," I told myself. Or was He really the one in control? Was He responsible for the many lonely nights of walking the city streets hoping to find my next hit of crack cocaine? How could I "let go," as Mom would say, when up to this point His power seemed too weak to keep me on track of serving him?

Was it His responsibility to forcefully change me or did I have any part to play in the process? I pondered restlessly with questions, hoping to find some answer. I found myself as this child again, looking for his daddy's hand, hoping to laugh again, as I remembered doing when Geggy and I played football in the streets. Again, life was a drag and I wasn't happy living in it. Yet I was too afraid to leave it.

I appeared in court the next morning ready to pay whatever the requested bond imposed would be. I made arrangements with my other partner to meet me there so he could assist with the bond payment. He was skeptical, stating how he believed going into a courtroom was taboo.

"Nonsense," I told him, "it's all in ya head!" The courtroom was fairly empty, which was a good thing because I wanted to get out of there as soon as possible.

I took a seat closest to the front, in order to provide him a better chance of seeing that I was there. I wrestled with my own apprehensions about being there, wondering if the same people that had arrested him were in the courtroom, and would they afterwards come for me?

He appeared in front of the judge wearing the same clothes he had been arrested in the night before, I suppose. I don't believe he noticed me because there was no indication. I scanned the courtroom, looking to see the identity of the arresting officers. Suddenly, I noticed a Mexican-looking man along with a short African American male walk towards the podium where "C" was standing.

While they were enroute, the Mexican-looking gentleman stared in my direction, as if we were rhythmically connected. Our eyes met. We gave each a stare as if to say, *I'm watching you*! That made me nervous. I wondered if they had any knowledge of why I was there. "Of course, they know," I said to myself. "The confidential informant gave them everything they needed." From that moment, I was ready to leave the court room. Whether his bond got paid or not, I didn't care, I wasn't trying to go to jail, was the only thought going through my mind.

I knew it was time to stop running. I had never completely stuck it out—trusting in God, that is. It was time I gave it all I had to give, reasoning within. I figured that if they had him, then it was only a matter of time before they'd be kicking down my door. I couldn't afford to let that happen. I didn't want to leave my son. He was four years old now and needed me. "He needs his dad in his life, especially now," was all I could think. Besides, I was thirty-one years old now, and really didn't care to spend the rest of my years behind bars.

I sat in the courtroom waiting to hear what the bond would be. Then it came. "WOW!" I gasped, "Three hundred fifty thousand dollars?… cash?!" repeating to myself what the judge had said to make sure I had heard correctly. "I don't have any portion of that," I said to myself. I knew there was nothing I could do for him. "If it's dependent upon me to ante up that much money… I'm sorry, but it looks like he'll be in there for a long time," I said, as if I was speaking to someone else. I surely didn't have that kind of money. And even if I did have that type of money, even ten percent of it, I couldn't pay it without having verification of a job. They would have arrested me simply to do an investigation.

After I had heard that horrendous bond amount, I took one last look around the courtroom. I noticed there were detectives watching me, but I was careful to keep my poise. Once out of their sight, I knew I was going to pick up the pace, changing my stroll into a mild trot.

While driving home I couldn't suppress the thoughts about the guy I thought I knew being an informant. The more I pondered on the matter, the angrier I became. "Mark told me that he was his brother," I said, holding a conversation with myself. My anger had turned into rage.

I reached my home in record timing. Instantly, I went into my office area, grabbed the business phone, and in a manner of thrusting the buttons, dialed the telephone number of his work place. The voice that answered the phone, giving the preamble to their business, brought a sense of calmness. Immediately after the soft music stopped playing and the receptionist began to perform her duties, I shifted into my professional mode and requested to speak to "L."

"Hold on one minute while I page him," she replied.

"This is "L,"' were his first words.

"Hello, 'L,' this is De'Ron. I need to see you."

"About what?" he asked.

"We'll discuss it when you get here," I said, trying hard to hold in the frustration.

"Tell me what it's pertaining to," he insisted.

"Listen, man, tell me the truth: are you an informant?" I asked straightforwardly.

I heard the drop in his voice from the next sentence he spoke.

"You know what happens to informants, don't you?" I continued to press him.

"I'm not an informant!" he insisted on saying.

"All right, then," I said, "If you're not an informant, then come to my house after you get off work, but if you are … then you have to pay the consequences."

"De'Ron, let me call you right back," he requested.

"All right, Holmes, but if I don't hear from you, I'm gonna take it as if my assumptions are correct, and the price has to be paid—in full!" I mentioned, hanging up the receiver on that note.

Immediately, I returned to the living-room area of my apartment. Feeling as though I needed some soft music to help me relax, I fell to my knees to be at the same height as the cassette player for easier access. I managed to take a quick glance upward at my coffee table, the place that contained the Bible I'd always open and close abruptly. Flipping a few pages, as always, I landed on a scripture that read, "Wealth gotten by vanity will be diminished." In a whisper tone of voice, I could hear myself say, "I always turn here. How do I always manage to go to this same scripture?" I closed the book after reading the scripture. Without rising from my knees, I slithered on the carpet to continue my first obligation, finding some music to soothe my troubled spirit.

Within five minutes from the time I had spoken with "L," I heard a hard knock on my front door. I could see through the door, for it was partially cracked. I wasn't sure who the men standing at the door were, but I could see that there were several. As I lifted myself from the floor to check to see who they were, I was hit in the face with noticing that there were five cars in front of my home. Two were unmarked and the others were cars that read "Deputy Sheriff." This was it, the moment of reckoning.

The first two men who stood at the door were wearing plain clothes. The others were wearing the typical police attire. I hadn't noticed at the time that there were also police officers and drug-enforcement agents standing guard at the rear of my home in case I tried to make a run for it.

The moment I showed my face to the officer, not opening the screen door in the beginning, the gentleman standing in plain clothes asked, "Are you De'Ron Smith?"

"Why? What's going on?" I asked, before I gave him anymore information.

It was obvious he didn't care to go through a dialogue. "Mr. Smith, may we come in?" he asked politely.

"Sure," I said. "What a dumb thing to do," I said to myself, after I had already given them permission. Once they entered, immediately they rushed me and began reading me my Miranda rights. I knew the Miranda rights by heart by now. "Stupid! Stupid! Stupid!" was all I could find in my vocabulary. This was warning number three, I thought, reflecting once again on Mom's emphasis on divine numerologies as they drove me downtown to the county FBI building to begin their interrogation.

I reasoned that this wouldn't be too hard for me to escape. They had nothing on me, I knew for sure. I had never conducted any business with the informant; therefore, I knew that it was mandatory for them to release me!

The interrogation process started the moment we arrived at their office. The officer chosen for the task to play "good cop" began. He came across as wanting to be my friend. The officer playing the role as "bad cop" stood by watching with a more serious look on his face. I won't lie, I was terrified. The good cop stated that I would be going away for a very long time if I didn't comply. "Comply with what!" I exclaimed. "I don't know anything!"

They presented many offers, inciting that I help them set up some of the other guys out there who were in the same type of business. For a brief moment, their offer sounded tempting. I couldn't see myself out of Jibri's life, especially for the length of time they were talking. "Life!" I said, jumping from my seat.

They continued to show me photos of guys from my neighborhood, asking if I had ever done business with them. I stuck to my story. I guess they were becoming frustrated with me and felt they needed to use more ammunition. The officer went to my wallet and retrieved the picture of Jibri. Apparently, they had been watching us for some time in order to know of my affection for my son. As soon as the officer opened the wallet and pointed to his picture, he repeated for the second time that I would be leaving him for a very long time. I broke. The mere thought of that occurring brought tears to my eyes. I stared at his baby picture in the wallet intensely before replying, "I don't know what you want from me; I don't know anything."

Now they had me and my partner "C" in custody. I wondered if they had made the same offer to him. I had nothing to exchange for a deal; therefore, I considered, if my freedom was dependent upon that, then I would be spending a lot of years in prison. I gave my last thought in defeat.

I hired the former attorney I used on my gun case because of the outstanding job he did defending me. I had confidence in his ability. But this time, I had no knowledge that he was fighting for his own freedom, as well. It was never mentioned by the judge that this attorney was wanted on charges of negligence for failure to pay child support, along with charges for probation violation. Because of his own pending charges, he made a deal with the very people I was fighting against for my freedom. He knew that I was innocent of the accused charges, but figured if he could count the courts a major player in the game, then his own buttocks would be spared.

He never answered any of my phone calls. And whenever I attempted to contact him, after Mom already p a i d him a retainer fee, he disregarded her efforts the same way. Mom even contacted the judge, informing him of my attorney's negligence towards my case. But none of them cared; they already had plans up their sleeve. I was to be their scapegoat.

Once I learned that information—three years later, I might add—I thought, "How could our judicial system allow an attorney to continue to represent someone when he himself is a wanted fugitive?" I was floored when Mom sent me the news clipping stating that he was a "Cincinnati's most wanted fugitive."

"He got what he deserved!" I said with great satisfaction.

I fought hard to save my janitorial company while in custody at the county jail. Daily, I called my home where my niece Monique acted as my secretary. She did her best to assist me, but the months of neglect and personal presentations that needed to be conducted pushed future customers in other directions.

After many efforts of sorting through plea agreements, hoping

I could receive something that wouldn't carry as much jail time as the agents had stated, and after signing bogus papers from the shyster attorney, I came to my decision that I no longer wanted him anymore to represent me. He had sold me down the river, in order to save himself, my cellmate told me. I was forced to fire him and find someone else to represent me. Mom and I did just that, but by the time she came on board to represent me, my former attorney had made such a mess of the case that the judge denied me the right to withdraw the bogus plea induced by the crooked attorney. This was a plea suggesting that I take a deal for a seven-year prison sentence. The original prison term consisted of twenty to sixty-eight years behind bars. "What man lives that long?" I thought. My new attorney did everything she could to prevent the inevitable. I had gotten caught up in the crossfire of someone else's deal to turn informant, and they had me.

There was nothing either she or I could do; prison was going to be my nesting place for a very long time, to paraphrase the words of the detective. "I hadn't done anything wrong," I confessed constantly to myself. "I was railroaded." Unable to comprehend the fact that I was on my to the Ohio Department of Corrections and my partner wasn't, all I could remember from the courtroom experience was turning around to notice the look on Mom's face when the judge handed down the seven-year sentence. We both immediately received revelation that God was in the midst of this. The mere fact that seven had always been her favorite number in reference to me provided assurance that, indeed, God was in this!

The acceptance of that revelation didn't make the fact that I was headed to prison any more comforting. It only served as an instrument assisting my understanding. What was I going to do? Furthermore, how could I possibly survive in prison for seven years? All I did was question why.

My conclusion was that I had to do this God's way. I was thirty-one years old and had lived life my way for the last time. I had tried church many times, to no avail. But I had never tried holding onto Jesus at all costs. I figured that if I was going to survive the life behind bars, it couldn't be done without Christ. I knew it was my responsibility to hold on to the promises I had made, with every fiber of my being. Thus, I also knew that God would have to prove Himself faithful in my life the same as I heard mention from other ministers and ordinary people who shared their testimonies. He would have to prove to me that He is a way-maker! A lawyer! A comforter! A provider! And a healer!

There could be no omission of either of His titles on my behalf, or else I knew for sure that I could never testify with the confidence needed. Neither could I walk in total faith. On this journey, God would have to appear in my life like never before!

I did what was required of me at the county jail while waiting to be transported to prison. I studied with the men, conducted bible studies, counseled those having emotional issues, and faithfully read the Word. I decided that if I was to gain any form of biblical understanding, my first responsibility was to begin reading, from beginning to end! I took the initiative in doing my part. Immediately, I knew I had to let go of any anger and all negative characteristics, just as the Bible commanded. This process called for the redevelopment of my mind and heart. I was ready this time—for real.

I told Mom that I wasn't going to return home with the same crazy thinking I had before I left. I was determined to return a completely different man, one way or the other. But it was all dependent on how the Lord worked in my life while inside the prison. Either I was coming home changed for good, or if He hadn't provided what I was looking for I was coming home changed for the worse. One way or the other, I was coming home different. My decision was final!

It took ten days before they called me to pack up my belongings and prepare to dress out for my departure, headed for my new residence for the next seven years. The announcement I'd been waiting to hear came by way of the cell intercom. Following the first announcement, an officer reiterated that it was time for me to report to the hallway to receive my white jumpsuit, designed specifically for individuals enroute to penitentiary. No one ever hoped to make it this far; this was the level everyone tried ambitiously to avoid. Unfortunately, my cards called for me to see this day.

My "celly" and I spoke until it was time for me to depart. He still hadn't gotten over the shock that I was actually being sent away. He was well versed in the law and had advised me to do certain things, but I failed to listen to his advice. Had I listened, I know very well that I never would have seen one day in prison. Nevertheless, when God has a plan for your life, "can't no one stop it," I came to learn.

I asked God to help me, I recalled saying. Many times, I awakened in sweat from horrendous nightmares of people returning from the grave who had overdosed on the cocaine I sold them. Whether directly or indirectly, I was responsible, I realized. Now it was time to take responsibility for my actions. My first step in change, I believed, was to be honest with myself. I did play a role in drug trafficking. Even if I hadn't sold drugs to the under-cover agent, I played the game; therefore, I must accept the consequences, reflecting on the most rational explanation possible to prepare me mentally for the journey.

"Everyone heading for the Ohio Department of Rehabilitation and Corrections, report to transport," came from the early-morning guard who popped his head in the living unit for that purpose only. "It's time to go to your new homes," he continued saying with a smirk on his face, as if what was happening held some sort of humor to it. I found absolutely no humor in it. I was leaving Jibri for a lot of years and at this point, I was ready to hurt anyone who perceived this as a joke.

I couldn't explain the mysterious circumstances that led up to this point. My heart was heavy with grief from the life I was living, I'll admit. And I did pray sincerely for all this to end, that too I'll admit. So, why should I be surprised at how it ended? I thought, trying to reassure myself and justify the end results. Otherwise, I knew that if I didn't view this as some sort of divine intervention, I would literally implode or go absolutely crazy.

I really didn't care to make my prison term difficult. The war stories I heard and read about that went on inside the much larger camps, I knew I couldn't take part in. I was nobody's chump and knew that if someone tried to violate me in any manner, my stay would be a hard one. It was my time to walk in my purpose, I supposed.

The new feeling of uncertainty produced the remembrances of Mom's favorite saying to me as a child, "This is my number seven child, God's perfect number." That quote rang louder in my head than ever. Although the vision of seeing anything other than a dim present over-powered me; I submitted to her prophetic words and managed to make-way with a smile.

Hazily, I stared out of the window as we traveled, fighting the fear trying to entrap me, adjusted my body in the seat for the most comfortable position, and in an instant, gave way to the journey ahead.

BECAUSE OF MY ACTIONS
PRISON LIFE

IN 1999 I entered the Ohio Department of Rehabilitation and Corrections reception center. It wasn't a shock to me. I was familiar with the protocol and procedure that took place upon arriving. But this time would entail a much greater discernment as to the actual meaning behind the front of "rehabilitation"… **CASH!**

Immediately the process of deprogramming began. Instantly I listened to the guards talk to you as if you were the lowest piece of trash on the face of the earth. Then, in their most demanding voice possible, commanded one by one to have a seat in the barber's chair. Beginning with those wearing dreadlocks, braids in their hair, and/or any type of fade, they were vindictively sought out, the sole purpose being to remove any form of self-identity.

As I watched the barber proceed with their instructions, I couldn't help but notice the expressions on each gentleman's face. They staggered in disbelief as they stared at themselves in the huge mirror, I believe put there deliberately to let us see that we had no say in what happened to us; all that was known of them—gone. And now, their only hope of identity lay at the base of the floor, waiting to be swept away by the first porter to arrive for cleanup.

In addition, the deprogramming and reprogramming works in contrast; that's designed to *conform* instead of *reform*. The goal is to erase any former hope, logic, or reasoning, and inject the characteristics of usefulness and lack of self-worth. The conclusion? To demoralize you, sending you back into the world worse off than when you entered the system. What a scheme.

As for me, this journey would be a method used to strip away any of my own self-righteousness and understanding and endow me with divine qualities. This journey would bring closure to any incredulous thinking I may have once entertained.

THE TRANSFORMATION BEGINS

AFTER we all had received our identical haircuts along with our clothing issue, we were escorted by an inmate to our individual housing units. The dorms were fairly small in comparison to some I had seen. These were mainly holding tanks until you were assigned to your actual prison camp. Each housing unit consisted of cellblocks. Rarely were there units permitting individuals to sleep in the bay areas, unlike when I first came through the system. There were people sleeping on top of each other—literally. However, this time it was different. The government had cracked down on overcrowding and began issuing fines if they came in and found individuals living outside of a cell.

Your day consisted of being locked away in your cell twenty-four hours, to exit only for breakfast, lunch, and dinner or an occasional one-hour recreation, if you earned it, for good behavior. There was no discussing whether you went to any of the mealtimes; it was mandatory. You had no voice. In fact, your only form of identification came by way of a six-digit number written on a plastic badge that had to be worn on a particular part of your uniform collar. It gave the environment an even more robotic structure.

I was appalled at what I was now witnessing: men at all times of the day, and even at night, herded like cattle to and fro. It could have only been God who pierced me with spiritual insight that would be my only hope of escaping such sinister surroundings. There had to be some sort of light at the end of this dark, dark cave, I thought. The negative environment attempted fiercely to force itself upon me in hopes to make me believe that this was my reality. "This is how it is, and this is how it's going to be ... conform or else!" is what the environment produced.

I was soon escorted to my lodging place, the place I would call home until my departure, cell number 1012. Upon entering, I noticed immediately the filth on the floor and the smoke-stained walls badly plastered with the remains of dead flies. "Am I really here?" I asked myself. I moved over to the window that had thick bars with little space between them to prevent anyone from escaping, and quickly fell into a daze. My eyes pierced through the thick bars at my new world. I tried to control the landslide of emotions, but to no avail. I was hurt … miserably in pain. My choices had landed me where I sat. And if things were going to change for the better in my life, then my upcoming choices would also take me to another place, somewhere more positive, I believed.

I continued to gaze through the thick cell window bars. The only place I could look was out at the fresh-cut grass and the trees that were beginning to shed their leaves. I had to accept the fact that I was indeed in prison and that I would be here for a very long time. I disconnected myself from the hypnosis, sat on the rack I used as a ladder to look out the window, and in one motion, indecisively opened my Bible to a passage from the book of Job that read, "What I fear the most has come upon me." I meditated on that scripture for quite a while. There was no doubt that I felt abandoned. I had left everyone and everything that held importance in my life. But it was about me now, and others like me, and the choices we make. Greed and lust for money and material possessions, in this case, were my curses.

It wasn't long before I was no longer the only person in the cell. Shortly after my arrival, though allowing me enough time to let my current situation absorb, a young man around the age of twenty-four entered. This was his first time in prison. I thought to myself, "The last thing I needed was to be housed with some nagging, bebop youngster who wanted to cry all night because he lost his girlfriend." I was caught between my own troubled emotions; therefore, I had no intentions to engage in any counseling session.

My first day was exceptionally long. I was completely exhausted from the 4:30 a.m. wake-up at the county justice center, not to mention the two-hour bus ride to our prison camp, then the in-processing period that consisted of being strip-searched and standing around with a bunch of strangers in their birthday suits waiting to be examined by the physician. The humiliation was repulsive.

As I began reading, along with taking notes pertaining to things I could understand, I noticed the young man staring at me. I couldn't help but notice his pathetic countenance. "He truly did lose his best friend," I said to myself, still vowing not to engage in any counseling session. He made it impossible for me to dismiss his sad projection. Occasionally he glanced at me as if to say, *please acknowledge me.*

The room maintained a bleak ambiance. Inside, there was nothing but sorrow and depressive spirits. No longer able to resist, I started a conversation by asking him how he was doing. I knew I had started something that wouldn't be so easy to end. He was torn into pieces, I could see. I understood partially; after all, I too had been young and fresh in penitentiary. I also remembered how lonely and fearful this place can be, including the fact of being away from loved ones and kids, if one had them—which he did, a beautiful baby girl not more than two years old. I have to say, that bit of knowledge changed my whole demeanor. I had also left a loved one behind because of my actions—my three-year-old son, Jibri. Soon, I was counseling a wounded soul, after all.

We conversed for hours, and the more we talked I found

I was beginning to like the young man. He possessed a genuine quality about himself, which told me from experience that he was different and had only managed to make a bad decision. Unlike me, who chose to do wrong for the sake of greed. But he wanted to fit into a lifestyle where he hadn't really belonged. I couldn't foresee him ever again returning to prison.

The lights were out at 9:00 p.m., sharp! This was to tell everyone that our day had ended. That indication meant that it was time for bed and that there better not be any noise heard when the correctional officer made his nightly round. A few moments passed before we each fell in silence, partly to allow the other time to grasp hold of his new circumstance, but more so to meditate on the errors made and to figure out a plan of how you would one day correct it—once given a second chance.

I requested to stay at the reception center because of the low number of inmates housed there, and because I knew I would be in a lot of fist fights at any other camp due to my current temperament. I was angry, and all it would take to set me off was for some tough guy to mouth off or approach me negatively because of my size; then I would have been serving life. "It's best I stay at this camp for now," I told myself.

It took approximately ten days before I received word of my acceptance from the camp's unit manager. For the first few weeks, I worked as a dorm porter. That meant I had to clean the living units; however, within my third week as a penal institute resident, I was called into the office of the gentleman who handled job assignments. I knew for sure that my level of prestige would ensure me a job of honor. After all, I was CEO of my own company, a counselor, and a store manager … I was a shoo-in, I figured in my arrogance.

I sank in disbelief when the sergeant announced my duty assignment. "What?" I said, "The kitchen?" I was angry, but I knew I couldn't reveal that emotion for fear of being escorted to "the Hole," the place for disciplinary people. It wasn't enough that I was wrongfully incarcerated, I thought, "But now, I'm made to go wash pots and pans bigger than me! Hell, no!" I exclaimed, but where only I could hear it.

It was 4:00 in the morning when I heard a tap on my cell door. "Get up!" the correctional officer exclaimed. Then, as if he was coming into my cell to physically wake me up, I heard keys being inserted into the keyhole. By his constant disruption, he awakened my cellmate, a brother from Dayton, Ohio named Frank. Frankie J. is what he went by, a good brother whom I h a d met at a dorm Bible study that he was conducting.

After attending several of his Bible studies and seeing that he was sincere in what he was doing, we connected. After sharing our stories with each other and learning how we both shared the eager desire to turn our lives around, we both came to the conclusion that we could benefit from each other. We had a lot in common and believed that we could help each other achieve what we were looking for out of life.

The fact that I was made to wake up at 4:30 a.m. was upset- ting. My deepest sorrows and regrets came mostly from the first morning, reporting for work in that dreadful kitchen. I sat and listened to the early morning conversations from guys who appeared to have felt right at home. I was disgusted with the entire situation. I tried to convince myself that I didn't belong here, comparing myself to the others. I needed to make some changes in my life, I knew very well, and this was going to be my starting place. I hated the kitchen; this was the workplace where people went who couldn't follow rules. I fit right in, I suppose.

My first thought was to refuse to work. I needed some rest badly but knew that I would be sent to the Hole if that happened. Although the consequences would be severe, I was willing to take the risk. "I had it with the kitchen!" feeling every bit of the hatred inside. However, the thought of refusing to work passed rather quickly. The more I thought about the punishment I'd receive, the more the kitchen didn't seem like a bad place to work after all, I convinced myself.

Instead, I decided to request to speak with the chaplain. This was an idea from another inmate. He said that if I told them that I was having problems dealing with prison, then the institution would authorize me a counseling session with the chaplain. I considered the idea and rushed to impose my desire on the kitchen supervisor. He agreed.

The timing couldn't have been better. There he was, the prison chaplain, walking directly in front of me as soon as I exited the front doors. I sprang in motion to catch him, hoping he'd have time for me to discuss my problem. He seemed a bit hesitant in the beginning; as I further explained, he suggested I follow him inside. I took a seat in the leather chair facing the window in his office. Outside I could see men walking or jogging around the makeshift track. He noticed my dismal stare. "What's the problem?" he asked.

Before I could even explain, my eyes filled up with tears. I began to explain about my case and how I was wrongfully convicted. My main objective was to share my feelings. I was becoming suffocated by the confinement. I needed a release valve, some way to release the pent-up frustration and anger dwelling in the base of my soul.

"Mom accepts all of my phone calls," I told him. "Had it not been for her, I don't know what I would do." She knew the strain of pressure I was under. And when we didn't talk by way of telephone, then I could look forward to Gail and my son Jibri coming to visit me at least once a month.

Gail stood in the gap. She allowed our once dilapidated relationship to grow into a mature brotherly and sisterly relationship. She came faithfully to visit me in the prison. She was the last person I thought would come bring me good cheer. I had hated her when we were kids, but now here she was, acting in   a loving and caring capacity ... you never know whom you'll need. That began to make me look at her differently.

I entered my first appeal for early release. All of the jailhouse lawyers said that my case was a shoo-in. That's what I needed to hear!

The new hope gave me enthusiasm, something to look forward to. From then on, I went to work diligently as instructed, even managing to wake up beforehand, motivated by the jailhouse lawyers' assurance of my freedom. I meant the vow I made and would do whatever it took in order to carry it out, I told myself.

Three months passed and still there was no response from the courts in regard to my appeal. I was becoming frantic, and the negative thought pattern that always assures you the worst has happened taunted me. However, not long after I returned to the barracks after a day's work in the kitchen, ready to go into my cell, the news came for me to report to the guidance counselor to receive "legal mail."

"This is it!" I told Frank. "This is the news I've been waiting to hear … be in prayer!" I said as I rushed to see the counselor handling my document.

Everyone who has ever waited on legal mail pertaining to their case can relate to the churning of the stomach and the butterflies that accompany the nervousness. Part of me didn't want to even open the letter. My first thought was to ask Frank if he would do the honors. "I have to see what is inside," I thought to myself. "Even if it's bad news, I would still like to know," was my thinking.

Slowly I opened the letter from the court of appeals. The very first line read, "Sorry …"

Immediately I gave-way to depression. I continued reading the letter in more depth, looking for the explanation that could tell me why the courts denied my appeal.

I was angry, for real this time. "What would I do for seven years?" I asked myself. Slowly, I walked upstairs to my cell where I knew Frank would be waiting to hear my good news. The news was anything but good, I told him. In fact, I went on to say, "The courts denied my appeal." He was speechless. He could feel my hurt and disappointment; he stated that he would leave the cell to give me time to absorb the rejection letter. "Thanks," I said, "I need it." I wasted no time falling to my knees after hearing the door close behind him.

I had no choice but to submit. My energy level was being depleted from having to endure the negative environment. I tried to live a life of good behavior, but it would have been easier if I simply allowed myself to react like everyone else. But I wanted to change, and that meant that I must learn to "think" differently. No more could I throw childlike tantrums when things didn't go my way. It was time for me to grow up, to become a man of God first, then a man for society, without forgetting how to become a better father for Jibri's sake. I missed him dearly, and knew he deserved the best I could give him. The first words to come out of my mouth were, "Why, Lord?" I had no idea how I was going to do this time. I cried harder, agonizing over the thought of having to press my way through each day. "To do one day in here is hard enough; how am I supposed to do seven years?" I abhorred this life inside prison walls. They treated us like animals and displayed absolutely no concern for our medical condition or welfare.

In fact, they buried anyone who died and had no family member to claim the body in a grave located in the rear of the institution. The environment induced depression. If one wasn't spiritually grounded, then he would easily fall into the trap of the system, sending him back into the world worse off than when he entered the system. But this was my training ground, the place where I could regain all that was lost … my purity … my innocence.

I stayed at the Reception Center as a *cadre* for one year before deciding it was time to move on to another phase. Frankie J. had already put in for a transfer to another institution and suggested that I do the same. He stated that the change would do me some good. I took his advice. I was told the transfer would take approximately forty-five to sixty days—that is, if granted. They had the option of denying a person's transfer. Oh, how I prayed that wouldn't be the case. I was sick of that place and agreed with Frank's suggestion, I did need a change.

My transfer papers actually came in less time than speculated, approximately thirty days, I believe. I was excited and looked forward to the new atmosphere. I wasn't sure what to expect from the new camp; all I knew is that I was more than ready to leave the nightmare camp in which I was currently housed.

Here comes God now

THE new camp was huge. The dreary building gave the impression of some sort of scary, hard-core prison movie. I was certain this was going to be a place where I'd encounter more time on my sentence.

It didn't take long for me to settle in. My first goal was to find the chapel … well, actually, it was to find Frankie J. I discovered my primary objective, and within hours we both were fellowshipping just like old times in the sanctuary. We developed a "praise team" consisting of four of us: Bill, Al, Frank and I. Then there was the intercessor who kept us in line, named Rex. Frank had this choir harmonizing. I never held a decent note before, and now I was singing in front of people. My life was being transformed right before my eyes. I wasn't the same person, this I knew. This time, something inside my heart was different; this time, I wasn't playing church.

I had been at the new camp for approximately nine months before I noticed my body beginning to go through changes. Out of nowhere, I began to struggle just to make it to praise team rehearsal. I was having trouble getting out of bed and could hardly walk across the compound. If I did walk, it was at a turtle's pace. I had no breath. For some reason, I couldn't breathe. This scared the daylights out of me. "Is God testing me?" I asked Frank. My breathing was getting worse, so I requested to go see the doctor.

I knew something was happening to me. The doctor suggested that we take some X-rays. He took a few of them, I recall, in hope of discovering whatever was ailing me. I wanted the X-ray reports to return quickly. The doctor said he would notify me when the tests results returned. In the meantime, I had to endure a failing respiratory problem and put all my faith in Jesus, like I said I wanted to do.

This was a test for sure. I had no appetite, which added to the rapid reduction in weight. I was becoming skin and bones; I hated to look at myself in the mirror. I was being stripped to nothing, I believed. And at the time, I couldn't understand the purpose behind it. But there was a purpose, a purpose much larger than my little mind could conceive. For now, I must walk by faith.

"It's not enough that I have to dress identically with 2500 other men; now I have to endure the public humiliation of looking as if I'm smoking crack or dying from AIDS," I said, unable to suppress the anger anymore. I could no longer act as if everything was okay; it wasn't. I was dying, I thought. "Where is God?" I released my pent-up frustration to my praise team brothers.

Unexpected News

THE X-ray reports returned to the infirmary on a day when I was right in the middle of praise team rehearsal. Apparently, someone from the infirmary called the unit attempting to locate me. There was no doubt where I would be. Everyone in the dorm who knew me also knew that I spent most of my time in the chapel.

The dorm officer who received the instructions to tell me to report to the infirmary called the chapel. Upon hearing the news to report to the infirmary, immediately that old bubbly feeling leaped in my stomach. I feared the news I was about to hear. I knew very well that in order for them to track me down the way they had, things had to be pretty bad.

Hesitantly, I moseyed to the place I didn't care to go. I thought it would soothe me if I indulged myself in an in-depth conversation with God. I knew this journey entailed dealing with my faith; I had very little. I kept right on strolling … slowly, I might add. Maybe it was the fear weighing me down that impeded my movement. I didn't want to hear anything negative. Truly, I didn't think I could bear it. I had a terrible vibe that there was some concern pertaining to my X-rays.

When I entered the building, the formality was to hand my badge to the correctional officer sitting at the desk located in the center of the hospital and wait for further instructions. It wasn't long before I was instructed to go straight to the back; after all, they were expecting me. Once I caught up with the X-ray technician, he stated that he needed to do another set of testing before the doctor could give me any conclusive information.

"What does he think he found?" I asked.

"I can't say; I'm not the doctor," he replied.

After all was said and done, I followed the same emotional proce-dure back to my housing unit to ponder on the test results and my failing condition. Mom was in need of knowing what was going on. I kept her up to date as to the progress or decline of my health. She was angry that nothing more precise had been done. I knew the process. Expecting an expedient turnaround from a prison wasn't possible. Their attitude towards us was, "Let 'em die."

A few weeks later, I was called into the medical office again, this time, to receive my final report, good or bad. I spoke with the same lab tech as before. Abruptly, the doctor interrupted our conversation, requesting to have a word with me regarding my test result. I sat in the seat waiting anxiously to hear his diagnosis. He marched through his original protocol before mentioning that a double set of testing had to be initiated because there was something strange about my first set of X-rays. He reached over to retrieve my medical file and, opening to the page that contained my results, he implied that I had a lung disease. I could hear nothing else from that moment. He pronounced the name of the disease, but it didn't matter; I was paralyzed. I had no idea what that word meant. Besides, it was so long of a word, I got lost at the first five letters. The doctor noticed my irritation. I didn't want to hear all of the medical terminology; I wanted to know if what I had was curable. I did ask him to repeat the name of the lung disease for clarity. In his old, native Pakistani accent, he squeezed out the word *sarcoidosis*.

"How did I contract it? Where does it come from? And, of course, is it curable? I let off a slew questions before he could answer the first one.

"Well, Mr. Smith, there are different levels of the disease, and right now, I can't say for sure if yours will progress," he said. The rest of the information I'd find out on my own.

Frank was waiting eagerly to hear the results of the test. Not far into my journey back to the dorm, I heard my name called. I wasn't sure from which direction it came but knew it could only be he, for no one else called me by that name. I motioned for him to come outside. The news was killing me; I needed someone who'd listen as I spilled from my heart about the anguish holding me captive.

He embraced me in brotherly affection and recited a few Bible passages to encourage me. He continued to assure me that God hadn't brought me this far to leave me. "It's all about faith," I whispered to myself, while laying my head against his shoulder.

"The battle is not mine—it belongs to the Lord," I quoted from a passage in the Bible. I estimated there was nothing I could do except pray and believe that God would heal me. I believed in Mom's prayers and her ability to get God to listen. It was my hope that even if God wouldn't heal me for my own sake, He'd at least heal me for the sake of Mom.

I was told it was necessary for me to transfer to another institution because my condition raised my medical level and that it was too dangerous for me to stay at the camp in which I was presently housed. I was told that I would be going to a medical camp, where I'd receive the treatment that I needed. Once the lung disease wasn't at such a serious level, I could return to my parent institution. All of us had become brothers, and I really didn't care to leave any of them.

I transferred to a camp that was mainly a camp for prisoners who were on their last leg of life. I believed I was dying, so for them to send me to this particular camp truly confirmed my suspicions. There is no fear like believing you are about to die. I didn't fear death itself but watching yourself die—that's another story.

It's time for my burial

AS soon as we pulled onto the location, I noticed men who were in wheelchairs. I hadn't fully entered the compound, so I was unable to possess a more in-depth view of everything, but upon doing so, we were immediately told to exit the bus. Shackled two by two, hand and feet, we looked at each other, wondering if we would make it out of here alive. I hadn't seen anyone in a wheelchair in prison before.

This was my third camp within two years. I was tired of moving around. The compound reminded me of the projects in Cincinnati. There were literally sidewalks and fire hydrants. This was no penitentiary, I thought.

The in-processing at this camp was brief and to the point. I liked that. But since it was after business hours when we arrived, there was no officer on site to issue our clothing. That was pitiful.

After the in-processing part was finished, we were instructed by the correctional officer to go directly to the infirmary. Once there, I stood in amazement at the sight! Not only were there men in wheelchairs, but blind and terminally ill individuals as well.

My white jumpsuit and bright orange shoes were an indication to the desk officer that I was a new arrival. He immediately pointed me in the direction of a congested waiting area filled with sick inmates. The sight was overwhelming, yet humbling. I observed intently men who were in far worse condition than I could ever imagine. These were men, young and old, plagued by incurable diseases. Many had severe disorders, illnesses that I didn't even know existed.

Within a few minutes of my stay inside the medical building, sitting on the hard metal slab they called a seat, I stared continuously in disbelief while the entire time asking underneath my breath, "Lord, am I dying?" The vague expression on my face served to anyone who noticed that I was saddened by the sight. I scanned across the room a bit further, not noticing before a person sitting directly in front of me. I couldn't tell if it was a male or female, but really, I knew—for this was an all-male camp— anyway, I noticed he was wearing a bandanna around his neck.

I wondered what his problem could be. Then, he managed to give way to a cough that provided the answer to my question. As he removed the bandanna, I noticed a hole in his throat. There was also a tube inserted—I suppose to block out dust or for allowing air to enter. I was completely ignorant. This was my first time ever witnessing a place where this could easily be titled, "the walking dead."

There came inside the infirmary a brother pushing an older gentleman who was also in a wheelchair. Immediately, I noticed something about the brother doing the pushing. I couldn't quite put my finger on it right then, but he wasn't your typical everyday inmate— meaning someone who looked for trouble or got involved in all sorts of unproductive activities. He displayed more of a calm spirit, sort of like myself or like the me I was working toward becoming. We had kind of kindred spirits, I could tell right off the bat.

When it was my turn to see the nurse, I rushed to inform him that I was a nonsmoker and I have a lung disease. The nurse stated that I was classed to another dorm, a dorm that was filled with smokers. "How can they send me to a smoking dorm, when I'm here because of my lungs?" I asked. The thought of going to the smoking unit made me sick to my stomach. Besides, I heard there were folks in there with AIDS.

I pondered on the news from the officer, then mentioned with more definitiveness, "I can't go to a smoking dorm; I have a lung disease!" He told me to let him check the records to see if there was something he could do. "He'd best do something," I said to myself while sitting on the hard seat, harboring mixed emotions of sadness and anger.

The guy who pushed the wheelchair and I formally introduced ourselves. "My name is Darryle."

"Hey, Darryle, I'm De'Ron," I replied. I asked if he went to church services held at the institution.

"Yes," he answered, going on to mention how good they were.

We came to spend a lot of quality time sharing and learning more about the word of God. I told him all about my brothers back at the other camp, whom I missed dearly. He had a flavor for sending off good vibes. His entire countenance was always at a level of peace. I liked being in his presence, and it was obvious he enjoyed the fellowship of our Bible studies together, often held in the quiet room.

This was an exceptional place to hold Bible studies. You could pray without any interruptions—that is, if it wasn't for the first-shift officer who resembled the lady from the movie *Throw Momma From The Train*. I don't know what I did to make her instantly hate me, but she vowed, "Before I retire at the end of the year, I'll have you put in the Hole!" This was her mission … and she pursued it diligently.

All of her attacks against me were extremely petty, but the purpose behind administering small tickets was to combine them. That way, the Rules Infraction Board (RIB) would find me guilty of having excessive tickets, no matter how small they were. She established a game plan beginning from my first week in her dorm. She stated, "You think you're better than everyone else!" This lady was crazy, I thought.

Daily she was sent "on assignment," I could only say, because there was no other way to explain her attitude towards me—she didn't even know me.

It became commonplace for the old lady to find something to tag on me. Each time she managed to do so, it resulted in having to stand before the unit sergeant to receive some sort of reprimand. I was in his office approximately two or three times a week. The first time in his office constituted of only a verbal warning. This was the beginning of her scheme.

Upon the second, third, and fourth go-around, things were beginning to escalate in the punishment area. I didn't feel I should have received any disciplinary actions to such bogus tickets, and I argued the fact. But what could I do? I was in their world.

The sergeant continued to act in a nonchalant manner whenever I argued my side of the story. He had the nerve to try and provide me with comforting words, before dishing out the punishment that was always in the old lady's favor. I knew there was no winning. He pretended to assure that "things will be just fine real soon." He went on to say that, "In a few weeks, at the end of December, she'll be retiring. Just stay out of her way."

"How do you suppose I do that?!" I replied. "I live in her unit!" I wanted to slam the door of his office but knew that wouldn't be the wisest thing to do at that point.

Darryle would always vouch for me, telling the unit sergeant that her ticket was fabricated. But we knew they would never take sides with an inmate, even if we were telling the truth. The sergeant knew there was nothing I could do to avoid the old lady. Part of his statement was sarcasm, I knew.

The old lady knew very well that the punishment for receiving a misconduct ticket ranged anywhere from commissary restriction to any number of days in the Hole. She also knew it would take time, along with many write-ups, before they would actually send me to the Hole. But she was on a mission.

Often, God will use a pressing method. God knew I still had a slight temper and issues with humbling myself to authorities. I truly believe now that He used her as an instrument to carry out His plan for my life.

Mom heard of everything that was happening to me at this camp. Mom and I both believed that possibly, since I was sick, it would carry more weight with the judge in attempting to have me released from prison earlier. We hoped that when it was time to file for another early release, he'd have compassion and grant it. It didn't work. For the third time, I was denied.

The tickets reached a new level and there were no words I could say to counteract their decision to put me in the Hole for fifteen days—the first time. And then, finding more things to add to my already messed-up disciplinary folder, she hammered me with a fight ticket, which also determined a mandatory fifteen days in the Hole. Ironically, this ticket just so happened to be heard during her final days working as a correctional officer.

She wanted every opportunity to see me placed underneath the jail. If she could have had her way, I would have been tied to a tree and flogged. Thankfully, it wasn't her call; however, the officers in charge of the RIB board knew she was about to retire and thought it would be good if they sent her off with one last granted wish: to see poor ole De'Ron sit in a dingey, hot, smelly cell for Christmas and New Year's. Her wish was granted.

She had been striving to see this day. She approached my bed area with a look upon her dull face of a child who had just done something she knew she shouldn't have done. In a steady motion, she walked directly to my bed area and told me to begin packing my belongings because I was wanted at the RIB board. "You know you're not coming back, don't you?" she said grimly.

"I really don't care," I replied. "In fact, if it means I get to be away from you, then I'll gladly go to the Hole," returning the same smile.

I had about all I could take of her. I was "ready to lay it down," as we say in the joint. I was willing, even if it meant nothing more than to find a moment's rest. All of my energy had been wasted trying to figure out a game plan to rebut her attacks. I wasted time fighting her in the flesh when the Bible clearly states that, "We war after the spirit."

I packed my belongings as instructed, often glancing at times to watch her parade around the unit like a jackal about to presume its kill. She gloated at my unfortunate position.

"It's okay, God has me covered," I said, looking directly in her dark eyes.

I taunted her, as well when I look at it. I knew she hated anything that had to do with God; therefore, I made extra sure to preach and speak about the Lord as much as possible, especially when she came in earshot. I was a bit passive-aggressive, I suppose. I had no concerns for her feelings. In fact, if truth be told, I would actually say that I hated her.

She sat in her black swivel chair resembling a troll on a shelf. I could tell she was itching to say something sarcastic when I passed by, headed to see the disciplinary board. She couldn't resist the urge. Her expression indicated that she was pondering exactly what she wanted to say. Then it came. Clearing her throat to ensure that I heard every word, she turned in my direction and said, "Goodbye, momma's boy," in her screeching voice, exposing the identity of her true character. I knew she disliked me, but never believed she actually hated me.

The feeling was mutual. The only problem was that I didn't have the fighting power. I was trying to fight a losing battle, I came to realize, and needed some intervention desperately. They seriously would have buried me inside the prison system, that much I was sure of. My lesson was to learn self-control, I believe, how to handle situations from thought, not emotions nor reaction. I needed to learn discipline. Serving God had nothing to do with my feeling, nor my emotions. She indeed was a test.

WHAT THE DEVIL MEANS FOR EVIL

THIS was my day of reckoning for the excessive tickets procured by Officer Black. I had no problem believing her unendearing pronouncement that on the day of her retirement I would go to the Hole. She had made good on all of her promises thus far, so I had no reason to doubt that this too would be carried out. They liked her, no matter how sinister she was—they liked her. And even if they didn't like her, they had to respect her. She had a bit of seniority in the system. Besides, every coworker knew that she didn't have a scared bone in her body. She even confronted the warden of the institution at one point in time and quickly came to learn that that was the biggest mistake of her career. She paid a penalty for that incident. She was ordered to perform gate patrol on her feet out in the cold weather. When I heard about that incident, I really had fun with her.

I stood in front of the RIB board ready to receive my punishment. It was expected that I serve time, everyone knew that especially for the fight. "It wasn't my fault; I told the Russian guy to stop picking on me," I told the RIB panel. "He followed me to each room; I tried to escape him!" I wasn't afraid of the little guy; everyone knew that, but I was trying to avoid hitting someone. I was trying to live a Christian life.

I answered every question pertaining to the circumstances that led me to see the board. They really didn't care to hear what I had to say, but it was a formality.

"Why didn't you just do as you were told, Inmate Smith?" one of the officers asked.

"I *did* do as I was told!" I replied, clearly exhibiting frustration through my facial expression.

As they proceeded with questioning regarding my behavior, I interrupted the speaker. "What is all the questioning for?" I asked, "You're going to do what you're going to do anyway! I'm sick of answering all of these useless and unnecessary questions …for what?!"

"Very well, Inmate Smith, please step outside while the board determines," he concluded.

I was about to sit in the Hole for a few days, I knew. Surely that performance would cost me time in the "think tank."

I stood near the door of the waiting area before hearing, "Inmate Smith," one of the panel members yelled. "Come inside."

I snatched open the heavy door. My bags were already packed, so there was no need for me to return to the unit. I knew I was here to stay.

"Do you have anything further to say before we hand down our decision?" the leader asked.

"No," I replied. "Just do whatever you're going to do. I've encountered the cells with hard mattresses, steel toilets, and no windows many times already, so what is one more?"

The loud noise inside the Hole always contributed even more to the already negative environment. What did I expect? This was the place where all of the behaviorally challenged inmates landed. I didn't believe I had a behavior problem, at this point. I thought I was here because some old lady had it out for me. But God knew that I needed work in the attitude department.

"Inmate Smith," he said, "You are to serve fifteen days in disciplinary control." I wasn't surprised.

Immediately after he gave his final words, I was escorted to the place where I'd receive my change of clothing. This was a uniform different from that worn in population. These outfits served as notice that you were being punished. Some outfits were orange and some were white, depending on the institution and the nature of your offense. There were even uniforms prescribed for folks who attempted to commit suicide and individuals with mental disabilities.

I followed the officer to my designated cell. "Just as I suspected: filthy!" I was the only one assigned to the cell at this time. That was always refreshing and a reward, especially since it was New Year's Eve. It was my desire to be before the Lord on my face, interceding for Jibri and my family when the New Year rolled in. But I never counted on being in the Hole. Nevertheless, the solitude provided just what I needed. For thirteen days, I stayed before the Lord. I wanted a breakthrough in my life and the cell, away from everyone, provided that opportunity. I understood that, "What the devil meant for evil, God used for my good!"

I reflected over the accounts of everything. I always did that. I sat upon the hard, steel rack lined with a thin slab they called a mattress and stared into space. "New Year's Eve," I said to myself.

The noise level from the other inmates in confinement was a sure sign that the New Year was fast approaching. I couldn't block out the excited cheers from those screaming, "This will be my year!" This wasn't my year, so there was nothing I could say. In fact, I still had approximately four to five years remaining.

There were even absurd shouts from the community homosexuals, requesting some New Year's company. Sadly, some were willing to accompany them if they could gain access to their cell. However, I was quiet as a mouse. To me, this was precious time, I believed, that the Lord wanted me to spend with Him. It was no fun spending the New Year inside of a dingey cell housed with fifty other screaming men. No, I would have preferred to have been at home with my son and my family.

I couldn't even make a phone call to my parents. This isolation was solely one-on-one time with God, I believed— time for me to reflect upon my negative attitudes and to realize that there are always consequences for my actions. It was time for me to submit to authority. I was obedient, but only if things went according to my favor. The lesson I needed to learn was true humility. Soon I'd be returning to my parent institution and knew very well that I had to change.

Confinement actually turned out to be the best thing that ever happened. I'm not saying that I would have chosen that route, nor is that the route required for everyone but for me, this served as a refining purpose. I needed the additional chastisement along with time to clearly evaluate my life and my destiny. Had it not been for the quality time, I'm almost certain that the hustle and bustle of the world and all of its fake idols would have undoubtedly sucked me under.

INNOCENCE RESTORED

I was recovering well and had gained all of my weight back and more. The doctors had given me a favorable report and reclassified my medical condition. The day was approaching that I could leave the nightmare camp and head back to my parent institution. I honored those who had prayed on my behalf and was sure that their prayers were a direct result of my healing.

I was "paying the price," as they say, for where God was taking me. If I had known what to expect, that my life would go this way, I would have committed suicide long ago.

Because of my new level of faith and new relationship with Jesus, my life had changed considerably. I made my decision to truly serve the Lord, realizing that everyone and every situation played a positive role in developing me into the man I am today. But it was my choice. God would never have done anything in my life, I believe, had I not fully surrendered.

It was my desire to do something different, to live differently, to act differently, and to make a difference. No longer can I see myself through negative eyes. I've learned to see the world through the mind of my heart. After all, "Whatsoever a man thinketh in his heart… so is he." I gave all I had to give in trusting God. It was my responsibility to believe He would do everything, plus more, of what He said he would do. My part was to obey and endure diligently. In the past, I had thrown in the towel whenever the fire became too hot. I had no intentions of hanging on if hurt as badly as they said it would. But now, my stance is indelible.

I'm honored that Dad managed to find his missing piece. Today our relationship is one that only God could have developed. He indeed is my inspiration and true model of a man of God. We're developing our relationship even more today. And through Christ, I'm confident it will continue to grow as a testimony for other broken father/son relationships. Have a little faith!

Cheryle (a.k.a. Bootsie), Debbie, Tim, Yvette (a.k.a. Lanny), Gail, Will III (a.k.a. Little Man), and my baby sister Sharon are also working to develop their relationships with one another, as well as with the Lord. I'm proud of them all! The willingness to allow the Lord to turn your life around takes courage. And even if it hasn't completely taken place, I have faith that it will. I haven't arrived yet. Not until the day of Jesus will I truly be able to say that I have arrived! So for now, I'll just keep on "pressing towards the mark!"

Only God can restore relationships, mend marriages, and turn a thief into an honest man. The world measures success by what a man can gain. God measures success by what a man can give away.

Everything I had to go through has been used for God's purpose and my good. The essential piece I've searched meticulously to find has been discovered. I have found my Father! And through it all, the intricate quality every child has a right to experience has been restored, the innocence of a child.

About the Author

A native of Cincinnati, Ohio, De'Ron Smith, born the seventh of eight siblings, is quickly entering the ranks of being called one of the most inspiring authors and speakers, as well as an intervention consultant specialist.

De'Ron, works diligently in his hometown as a mover and shaker of reformation for individuals encountering barriers due to imprisonments, drug addictions, or many other challenges that could hinder them from maximizing their individual potential and achieving their divine purpose,

His autobiographical book, *Innocence of a Child*, reaches beyond the barriers of race, economics, or gender, and is a great educational read for children as young as thirteen years of age.

Mr. Smith continues to establish himself through serving as an active board member of organizations and church affiliations that convey great passion for incarcerated individuals, as well as individuals fighting illiteracy and poverty throughout the crevices of inner cities. His works also include spearheading an LLC company that focuses on social skills, self-esteem, character development, behavioral modification, and life's choices throughout institutions, agencies, and the educational system. His new approach to intervention is receiving recognition; his methodology in assisting to restore fragmented lives is gaining request from professional educators looking to gain more understanding, a new way of communicating, and new ways of approaching their target audience.

Mr. Smith has been featured in newspapers, on the internet, and on radio stations that provide international coverage. He has appeared on multiple talk shows, is a recipient of the Ambassador for Peace Award (an international recognition) and has appeared at the

White House in Washington, DC for a roundtable discussion, sharing his autobiography, the effectiveness of his work as an intervention consultant specialist, and the effectiveness of mentoring.

De'Ron thrives on modeling what he preaches. As a licensed ordained minister, he's not hesitant to attribute all of where is today in life to God. His own life's story, he hopes, will serve as inspiration to many.